KEEPING HEART

POEMS 1967–89

KATABASIS

KEEPING HEART

POEMS 1967-89

by
Dinah Livingstone

First published 1989 by Katabasis
10 St Martins Close, London NW1 0HR

© Dinah Livingstone 1989

Cover illustration by Anna Mieke Lumsden
Distributed by CENTRAL BOOKS
14 The Leathermarket, London SE1 3ER
01-407 5447
Typeset and designed by Boldface Typesetters Ltd
17a Clerkenwell Road, London EC1M 5RD
01-253 2014
Printed by Short Run Press

ISBN 0 904872 11 14

POETRY BY DINAH LIVINGSTONE

1967   *Beginning*
1968   *Tohu Bohu*
1969   *Maranatha*
1970   *Holy City of London*
1971   *Captivity Captive*
1974   *Ultrasound*
1977   *Prepositions and Conjunctions*
1982   *Love in Time*
1983   *Glad Rags*
1985   *Something Understood*
       (All Katabasis pamphlets)

1987   *Saving Grace* (Rivelin Grapheme, London)

HER TRANSLATIONS INCLUDE

Karl Rahner, *Nature and Grace* (1963); Lorca and John of the Cross, *Poems* (1968); Georg Schäfer, *In the Kingdom of Mescal* (1969); Dorothee Sölle, *The Truth is Concrete* (1969); Wilhelm Weitling, *The Poor Sinner's Gospel* (1969); Alain Labrousse, *The Tupamaros* (1973); Helder Camara, *The Desert is Fertile* (1974); Ernesto Cardenal, *Love* (1974); J. Gelineau, *The Liturgy* (1978); J. Leclercq, *This Day is Ours* (1978); A. Pérez Esclarin, *Jesus of Gramoven* (novel, 1980); W. Beyerlin, *We are like Dreamers* (1982); C. Mejía Godoy, *Nicaraguan Mass* (songs, 1986); Ernesto Cardenal, *Nicaraguan New Time* (poems, 1988); *Anthology of Latin American Poets in London* (part, 1988); M. López, *Death and Life in Morazán* (1989); C. and L.E. Mejía Godoy and Julio Valle-Castillo, *The Nicaraguan Epic* (songs and poems, 1989).

ACKNOWLEDGEMENTS

Some of these poems have appeared in the following magazines and anthologies:

Acumen, Ain't I a Woman?, Agenda, Akzente, Angels of Fire, Apples and Snakes, Aquarius, Arc, Arts Council Anthology 1, Big Bang, Blatant Acts of Poetry, Camden Voices, Camouflage, CIIR News, Cobweb, Dancing the Tightrope, Eve before the Holocaust, Help, Janus, Libertad, Limestone, Mandate, Montage, New Christian, New Poetry, Nicaragua Today, Only Poetry, Oyster, PEN Anthology, Platform, PN Review, Prospice, Publishing for People, Spokes, Slant X, Strange Mathematics, The Tablet, Third Eye, Tranquillity Base, Transformation, Voices from Arts for Labour, Well Red, Workshop.

Poems reproduced from *Saving Grace* (Rivelin Grapheme, London 1987) are by kind permission of the publishers.

I'd particularly like to thank my proof readers Bryan Abraham, Sasha Baker, Helen Barrett, Cicely Herbert and Kathleen McPhilemy, and Dale Russell of Boldface for his insight and skill in designing this book to fit my poems.

CONTENTS

PROLOGUE
1989

RECALLING

That bitter winter
in the bleak north city
shortly before her firstborn
slipped into the world
with the skin of his face
shining from far
like a sudden moon,
like the gospel pearl,
the dayshift midwife bustled in
giving a first order to the man:
Light the fire!

The mother about to be
watched him kneel – at least today
no way can he make her do it –
and the jet coal glow vermilion
energy joy and pain.
Later came tea –
too high for bread and butter –
and on the snowy apple tree outside
a blackbird prophesied.
The room grew warm
and dreamy black and red.

EXPECTING
1967/8/9

NOW I'M THE GRANDEST
TIGER IN THE JUNGLE

We did not fear pain,
the flesh of proper patience.
We did not fear violence
on the night of revolution.

But on the morning
beginning our time,
hell to redeem,
we sat down to a sad pudding

still in the jungle.
It is fear,
little brother,
it is fear.

Because our action
was afraid to avoid
the alienation
of the dominative servile mode.

The prince of this world presided,
we sat in the mode
of his kingdom
and drank too much gin in his name.

Kyrie eleison.
Our strength is spent in vain.
It is fear, little tiger,
it is fear.

THREE WOMEN

'Believe me,' said one,
'I have given my strength.
There is nothing to me
but common emotion.
Warm olive oil
in a cast iron pan,
the abstract smell
of suffering humanity
thrilled me uncomfortably
as a well-heeled girl.
I wanted to join in.
I lost the thrill
when the difference went
between what was mine
and what was other people's.
My small contribution
has nothing intellectual
about it. I tend
my own hurt, serve my own
ends and would be lonely
in a hollow tree,
not that I am afraid
to rot with the wood
to bare my soul there,
not afraid of the smell, but
how futile.'

'Admirable, yes,
but I want
to write.
Let me be calm
to collect what I am
from the muddle and mess
du lieber Augustin.
How can I love
with nothing to bring?'

The sparrow hovered above.
It did not belong to the house.
It did not belong to heaven.
In exasperation
the gipsy woman
stood up like a thing possessed,
drank without pause
the fire water brandy:
sang with duende.
Her voice was the marvellous rose.
It could not last.
She came out of the house
for a moment, in from the cold
for a moment. She escaped
the choice, wanting not
one thing but all of it,
utopic and pure in heart.

NIGHT PRAYERS

Her old age
is waiting for her
at the bottom of her mirror.
So she says:
I am not my face,
I will find a lover
to love my soul.

Maybe she cannot control
other people
but really
God is more real
and he will always
work to rule.

Mirror mirror on the wall
answers her:
In evening pain,
remember Queen,
beware of human breath.
It can kill
a good death.

SEPTEMBER IS A CHILLY MONTH

Love ate a mango
at Hampton Court.
Did you ever have one
golden my dear?

Smooth a skin as his shoulder
who was a runner
and beautiful creature.

She bit her soft fruit
in the chilly September,
got a knowledge too clear.
Fear bought a jam tart.

HOUSEWIFE

I saw a tiger eating the washing
the poppy crumpled in my head
my eyes admired the broken shard
and I flattened my foot on the sweaty butter.

I found a dead baby in the dustbin
floating on the melting pool
spreading over all the floor
of tiger butter blood and water.

Bad day
got tea
for me
and the kids

moving about my dirty kitchen
with a body like jelly.
I only took it I still existed
because I saw the tea I had made.

GLASS WOMAN

1

And traffic
broke into
my brain
which is not hidden
but shaken
window.

I hold up my house
by my will.

I scream
this commotion
is alien.
I am
an inadmissible
claim to calm.

And the stress of my house
still has my will.

Our house is broken
my children.
My will
is not broken.
Something evil
has shaken my freedom.

2

The glass woman
in still night
heard the cats howl
at their black delight.
It is the pain
of her son.

The glass woman
feared the light.
At her call
the builders blot it out.
First explain
even to them her sin.

(Well fancy.
Fancy her?
She's ill.
Increase the bill.
Two please,
madam, in our teas.)

Yes my nylon
dressing gown
has pocketsful
of bloody cotton wool.
My selflessness
is the stuff of evil.

When the builder
finished her house
it did not cover
her nakedness.
Still he fancied a nice place
so he smashed her.

PICNIC IN ST MARTINS GARDENS

In the heat of summer
drink white wine
in the bonepit.
Let the children
drink a bit
and dance on the smooth tombstones.

Beware
the black and gentle cat.
He will get in
everywhere.
Never fear the dancing children.
Enter cat and take possession.

Stroke my bones with your furry fur,
gentle cat.
I was a woman, now I am warm again.
Eat my meat for your dinner,
gentle cat
and leap in the strength of the sweet white wine,

moon's father,
feline
on my tombstone,
nightmare
of my children,
heat of summer.

SHOPPING

Noise and ugliness
on Camden High Street
obliterate consciousness.
A proper sleep is fed
on poppies with the dead.

Shiny and flat
yellows
inside and outside
buttercup petals
still tell the sun
what he has done.

In green rain
bow down
before the glory
of upright corn,
eat bitter sorrel,
suffer my scarlet poppies.

CODEINE

I feel
lousy
when I get the curse,
a different person.
I suppose
it is still
me.

But if I kill
the pain
in drug and dizzy ways
I doze
in a submarine
daze
for days on anemone days.

And if I
don't try
to stay in control
my plans all fail
but fluid and pale
impressions
amaze me.

LACE CURTAIN

Not the busy stitching
necessary
to the pattern
of the curtain
but the interstices
that made the rose,
the slitted eyes
of complete exhaustion,
rainbow recovery
of purity
and smiling sensuality
without the plotted gin:
the unexpected peace
and rare gentleness
were the holes
in the lace.

THE NIGHT OF THE GREEN DRAGON

In the impossible night
the green dragon came to Camden
and got the girl.
He was thunder and hail.
How could she hold him?
He was the jungle vegetation
which sprang on her
before she could draw breath
and pressed down roots
into her goodness.
This was the justification
of all her waiting.
But the planting was an illusion.
He was the one green dragon
who ate her soul and floundered
out of Camden before the dawn.

The green dragon
went home to the tunnel,
which runs from the Roundhouse
to Euston Station
and his pace was the possible night

when two lovers who were old friends
returned to their neat conversion
in Albert Street,
and having nothing to say to each other
slept back to back.

In a cellar across the road
a girl with long hair
danced like Isadora
and crept out unaccompanied
because she could not consider
any of the men.

A mother struggled out of a dream
to suckle her tiny child.
Sitting bolt upright to keep awake
she smiled at his spit image beside her
who kept her warm as he slept.

The fuzz prowled on Parkway
in a rather pleasant mood
and a pale man smiled
at the green moon,
his only companion in Camden.

Cursing the traffic on the High Street
the Greek priest
dismissed his housekeeper,
combed his beard
and handled his pistol with secret pleasure.

Little Rita by the canal
wished her aunt and her mother
would not snore so loud
while she prayed for peace
and a garden.

On Primrose Hill a young Spaniard
made his thirtieth honourable proposal
to the girl of his choice
weeping so bitterly that she took him to bed,
dispatching him at last for good
with this consolation.

A five year old
who had started school that autumn
had fitful dreams
of his new best friend
who was much cleverer on the apparatus.

In his pristine flat
a man with perfect taste
sat alone with his reefer
and the Goldberg Variations.

The green dragon
came home to the tunnel,
which runs from the Roundhouse
to Euston Station.
He was not happy there
but it was useless pretending
he was a proper man.
He wanted a woman
to wait with him
seven years in the tunnel
until his time was up,
without once letting him touch her
or losing her temper.
He had not found
such a woman in Camden.

And anyway who could say
that on the day of his transformation
she would not prefer the dragon
to the new man, or he would not
want to escape such devotion
and make it with a slick chick
in Regent's Park in springtime
in the newly possible
languid afternoon?

MAKING GOOD

He takes responsibility
for the state of society,
to pull apart and understand,
undertake and bear in mind –
such a good mind – the structure
of our past and future.
Although he has not chosen
manual labour,
he is still a worker,
disinherited,
conscious of deprivation
and with the queer tool kit
of the intellectual
to his brothers answerable.
He has enclosed the hollow hurt
unfelt now and vacuum-sealed.
He works well and to our benefit.

Let it not cost
him all his joy,
although they have stolen
the earth away.
Let him tell wheat
from bearded barley,
bless rockrose and harebell
and actually dance not just
flog it as simile.
As he is passionate
let him trust delight
and let an undaunted spirit
sometimes have a rest.

ARCHDUKE TRIO

Do you like it?
I like it,
grateful to rest.
Remember this
music suggesting
terror would pass?

We did not believe it.
Now we are resting
it can suggest
terror
we barely remember.
We like it.

EXMOOR

UP DUNKERY

The dog rose was not weary
in its day.
Stitchwort wild and pale
consoled the afternoon.
Clearly the periwinkle
understood the snail.
Intelligent the scarlet
of the pimpernel.

And they screwed in the key of e flat.

Can cold divinities
of space and time
win and condemn
this conversation,
can it wait in peace
to overcome them

believing the future to be absolute?

Purest horses hammered that
dark parabola
in twilight pointed
by pedantic pines.
In the combe the tanners' oaks
praised the useful stream.
Sorrel-tasting waters ran
fast and musical.

Friends mend their ways, abide the open pattern.

I was afraid,
comrade,
of the imperfection.
But you understood
and came
and we had freedom.

Mortal bodies speak, expecting resurrection.

GREAT ROWBARROW

Harebell clear
under it
smooth body of heather
starry delicate
and the violent colour
get in
mother

rock me rock me
till I'm still
ease my bones
with your cool smell

an event
on grass eyelash thin
the occasional ant
or gorse pricking
my slit of sight
now appropriate
to a plant

feed my bones
now I am still.

IMITER LE CHINOIS

'la fleur qu'il a sentie enfant
au filigrane bleu de l'âme se greffant.'
MALLARMÉ

He painted one rose
on a moon white cup.
The flower was his
that grew in secret
since his only looking glass
was his mother's lovely face
mooning over his delight.
And the rose grows on his deep sleep.

PRAGUE ADVENT

The ample bland blond residence expands
mansions sufficiently under the sun
to command three paved courts' perimeters.
Walk through the tunnel to the inmost one,
and your eyes expecting ease
from the pleasing regularity of square or octagon
are shocked by the black and trebly high cathedral,
squatting hen and gothic on the yard,
happy as the uncouth coaltooth grinning giantess,
mother of all the living, on her birth stool
plumb in the middle of the yellow municipal flowerbed,
unaffected by the pleas for hygiene and tidiness
of the deputation of foolish burghers.

Under the ribs of stone
in her monster belly's red amber penumbra,
the dwindled canons sing evensong
for the twenty-first of December.
Three chant, one angrily drones
the Magnificat antiphon,
sharp and intentional circular saw,
gnashing his failing heart out in a harsher wail
than all the prophets of Baal,
a swoon pure plainsong
bitter orange peel oil
when the bottom teeth gently press it
not quite to the pith.

Saviour see daylight, be lovely daylight
to all of your own,
foetal prayer of a creature,
not quite a full stop on a typewriter,
to achieve bean size, seaweed hands, humanity:

Come sun of righteousness,
Daystar, splendour of light eternal,
give light to us sitting in darkness
and the shadow of death.

THE ESCHATOLOGICAL DIMENSION

Pregnant woman cannot reach her feet.
She is a barrel.
Her fellow carefully rolls her about.
He's in bed with a whale.
He likes her like that.

On a good day she can understand
the astonishing thought
that Origen taught
that glorified bodies are perfectly round.

ULTRASOUND
1974

Ultrasound is used to make pictures of unborn babies. And:
'Ultrasonic vibrations are used to remove hard calcium deposits from
the heart in a new technique devised by a London surgeon for
repairing leaky or narrowed heart valves. The first results with the
treatment reported in the *British Medical Journal* today suggest that in
some cases the technique may be a safer alternative to replacement of
diseased heart valves by plastic artificial ones.' *The Times* (28.7.72).

I LIE AWAKE AND THINK OF THE PAST

The incredible Bozle
remembered the day
she was born
how she had been
inside
before.

If she could talk
she could tell
how it is strange to uncurl,
and my own cry
is an alien noise,
I heard your voices
but not like this.
It was dark,
I somersaulted
but saw no faces.

Words will not come
to her aid
till odysseys after
she has forgotten
the feel
of that time.

ULTRASOUND

AT EIGHT MONTHS

Bounce off your bones,
sounds discern
your bounds unborn.
The rough picture
is a small human.
The hard skull
guards, the brain
already deals
with certain
dark sensations.

Later you tell others
who you are
in sounds you learn.
They assessing answer,
set you down.
May the brittle bones,
soft brain loaned
to definition
still register
rough possibles

ultrasound.

34

AT HOME

The infant howls
when she hears
her parents quarrel
in murderous
silences
and bears their woes.

The infant smiles
asleep and murmurs
simple rhythm
when she hears
friendliness
in the dark room.

Street market gluts
give cockney sounds
fruit and flowers
summer peaches
fur blushes
bursting honey
trickles golden
in the cleft between
round mounds
erupt benignly.
Infants want to live
and have acute desires.

AT HEART

Ultrasound disperses
the hard chalk blocking
the channels of the heartspring
and makes it well again,
heart of flesh.
Take away the stone.

Pick up sound and stresses,
minutely particular,
music of common detail,
how hardly acceptable
by my ear.
Let me now listen.
Take away the stone.

'We're both North Londoners,
born and bred, no longer young.
Once we went in
with a mate of mine,
partners in a general stores,
Lewisham way.
It might have been Ong Kong
or the jungle.
We couldn't stay.
We left the house and all
and went into rooms to get back here,
fast as we could, north of the river.'

If without gentleness
office or theory
dismiss this story
with its sisters numberless,
that throne, domination
is unholy and vain.

Why may not these two sit
by crimson fuchsias
in the memorial gardens
of Old St Pancras,
if those are the flowers
they care about
and they hurt no one?

Poetry is the human heart
which is not plain.
For All Cows Eat Grass
in the spaces of the bass
but in the treble, dear old FACE.
Let me pay attention.
Take away the stone.

PANCRAS AND KENTISH TOWN REPOSE

May the pillars of St Pancras
be golden
in ordinary sunshine
and the lambs not be religious
but laughing children,
O my white woolly one.

Let poetry be versed
in echoes from echoes
of the past,
in each word's ties
to mental passion,
take the weight, pity
the blood and death.
But let it not flinch
or lose its savour
to season the earth.

Let its minerality
be the undoing of religion,
the irony of ideology,
the moony halt,
the intelligent wrench,
the pinch of salt.

Let it speak fair
and be compassionate
but most praise
what is great and lovely
in spite, in the face
of everything,
the overcoming,

just as its own obstinate
force and lilt
conjures the darkness
of chaos with common salt,
the word of grace.

May the towers of St Pancras
be golden
in common sunshine
and our free running children
find grace and peace,
O my white woolly one.

BABBLE

Infants first encounter
their mother tongue
through rhythm
of a voice rocking,
through melody
of tone consoling.
They cry from natural hunger,
fear the doom,
but titchy young
they also cry of boredom,
crave society, listening
to their own wail,
practise phrasing
something musical.

I still find it astounding
that such scraps can indeed
reflect and be sad –
when pleased they gurgle
and thrill thrushly –
that language breaks out in song,
is suckled on poetry.

Learning to speak
they will mimic
sounds expressing
qualities of a thing
in a situation given.
They become intellectual,
concerned with sign
and relation,
wordgame and pattern,
but their hermeneutic
is never prosy;
it is a poetic.
Love is its meaning,
need for connection.

THE WELFARE

Today Mean Norm came
to check the children.
In my relegated holey
shortie nighties
I at the time
was flea killing
with my flit gun.
His greeting
was terse and bossy.
My ilcome was worse.
Mean Norm is an old enemy.
Genius he abhors,
of course, even oddity
he hates and fears.

Take your normalising,
social working, recording
hands off the children,
you bland sneak. Try me,
I guard them free,
I like them this way,
original and discrete
from you, from me.
If I am repellent
to you in this garment,
you are repellent to me
because you dole and deal
in the innocent,
frustrate their poetry.

Don't think you'll get
the children away by pleas
of maternal madness, Mean Norm.
Why should we conform
while we can still outwit?
Anyway rags are suitable,
right for the occasion,
as a lady should be.
It's sensible to sport
old clothes for hunting fleas,
useful to dress the part
for when I meet one
face to face, and now please
I suggest you flit.

THE FIRST DAY

And the rising from the dead
for the freedom of the morning,
while it was yet dark
in expectation of the morning.
The child is delivered
at breakfast time.
In England the mother is offered
a cup of tea.
The afterbirth is thrown away
wrapped in old print in the dustbin.

The dogs shall eat Jezebel
and every sacred idol
shall be broken down.
Construct and cling, conditioning.
What love makes is a lovely thing.
Let it not try to contain
what it breeds within. Break
out and shout, infant's breath
and the rising from the death
and the revolution of the stone
and the quitting of the tomb
very early on the first day.

BE NICE

If she sees a cripple
she cuts off her arm,
fearful
she will not feel
with him
unless she's the same.
That is practical.

If he sees a cripple
he locks him away
careful
the intractable
problem
should not spoil his day.
That is natural.

THE SOFA

The smug bien-pensant
trendist social worker
condemns the slightly affluent
young working class couple
for buying a two hundred pound sofa,
or rather monster three piece suite
in olive uncut moquette.
Wherefore was this waste
in such bad taste,
he cries, and you forget the poor?

I loathe the man's conceit.
I rage at his crassness.
For I know why I
have never spent more
than a pound or so on furniture.
My bones and blood
are at ease from centuries
of privilege and I can afford
shabbiness and eccentricity.

If I know, so should he
that this young woman
(she works in a typing pool –
he disapproves of her more
because she is fashionable
from a chain store)
may be the first in her family
since the Industrial Revolution
whose loveliness at seventeen
will not vanish in her twenties,

likewise this young man
wants them to have a decent place
when they marry, comfortable
with a bit of luxury.
Why shouldn't they?

Know-all social worker,
you and your politics
are unfit to rule,
unless you have sympathy
from the inside
with every human body,
desiring the shock beauty
of your own and the other sex,
because that is natural,
feel fellow with the ugly,
respect the wishes of the people.

One day perhaps this couple
will make love on their settee
and laugh when it smells to heaven.
Perhaps their children
will bounce on it and their pleasure
rate higher than furniture.
It will be scuffed with history
and then they may relax
and feel and be more free.

The Vanguard Party
which condemns uncut moquette
(because they would never want it)
is vile tyranny.

YOUNG COUPLES' DINNER PARTY

We're going out to dinner.
He comes in, reads the paper,
soaks in the bath, changes at leisure.
I make him tea, suckle the baby,
supper the toddler,
peel off my hugger-grubby skirt
for a new dress I made today.
You look horrible, he says. Tarty.
Wear something quiet.
I gulp and do it.
Won't we be late if we quarrel?
At the bus stop it starts to drizzle.
We wait. It pours. He blames me
for the slowness of public transport
and the soft depressing flood.
Do men think us all powerful,
that we control all fluid,
inhuman female wetnesses
and the tides of green buses?

We get there.
Pat between nursery and kitchen
swings monkey-like. Soon she'll be done.
The men liaise, fuse,
philosophy and poetry
off for a quick one.
Hours pass hungrily.
The food will spoil, Pat admits.
Couldn't we begin?
Is she going to cry?

Harsh her rush from work
to cook her birthday meal.
For that we wanted men.
Why? Open the wine. Cut the pie.
Damn them to hell the swine.
Oh how guiltily we guzzle, sozzle and giggle.
Don't grumble. Are we not
their easily removed appendices?
Girls know your place and purposes.

The men have arrived.
Well girl, where's the food?
Look sharp, poets Fred. We smile.
He lurches forward, lashes out.
Pat screams, I give her cover.
We cuddle, rather, sheeplike huddle,
both cry, kiss, cling,
mothering and babying each other.
Thus we baffle and appal.
The men rootle disgruntled, find bread,
eat with huge self-pitying greed.
We let them get on with it.
How disgustingly they masticate.
They pretend they are in control –
cool man cool, and silent –
but truly it's our little moment:
we feel closer and are better fed,
till the inevitable comeback come
and the grim-coupled journey home.

FEAR

Girls in your struggle
no longer to be
underbitches,
may I suggest some exercises
in moral courage.
First develop your
eccentricity and rage.
If phallic motor car
threatens your pushchair
at a zebra,
know how to swear
superbly. Take his number.
Try a retaliatory
water pistol
of indelible ink,
red for blood.
You must make a stink.

Fear in the pit
of the belly,
indigestion.
Fear on the tongue,
sharp and dusty
ashy onion.
Fear between shoulders,
clenched shrug-ugly,
ripple-whip-frozen.

Fear up my legs
turning to jelly,
contradiction
notwithstanding,
fear churning
the pit of the belly.
What terrror! I endure it
but what do I fear?

Choose a name
which pleases you.
It need not be your maiden
or your married.
You belong to no man
but by your own gift.
If you get tired of it
change it again.
Go to the bank, boss
or passport office,
alone and in person.
Keep calm.
If they put you down,
smile but insist
they do exactly
as you say.
Your name's your own.

Fear in the pit
of the belly,
indigestion.
Fear on the tongue,
sharp and dusty
ashy onion.
Fear between shoulders
clenched shrug-ugly,
ripple-whip-frozen.
Fear up my legs
turning to jelly,
contradiction
notwithstanding,
fear churning
the pit of the belly.
What terror! I endure it
but why do I fear?

Dress your scruffiest.
Blood on your skirt
if you like. Why not?
On a day when your hair
is at its mouldiest
go to Liberty's and try on
their two hundred quid dresses.
Don't tremble.
Speak as one
acquainted with luxury.
Be exacting and cool
as a millionaire.

Pile the clothes on the floor.
Leave without excuses.
Buy nothing. Be sure
not to fall for conciliatory
bamboo whistles at the door.

Fear in the pit
of the belly,
indigestion.
Fear on the tongue,
sharp and dusty
ashy onion.
Fear between shoulders
clenched shrug-ugly,
ripple-whip-frozen.
Fear up my legs
turning to jelly,
contradiction
notwithstanding,
fear churning
the pit of the belly.
Terror is past. I endured it.
What did I fear?

AN OCCUPATION

**Taking over Wasteland for a
Playground in North London**

And shall this London,
our capital city –
remember her citizens
blitz withstood –
and shall this London
whose civilisation,
piecemeal, painfully,
has a reasonable pride,
whose ancient accents dry and witty
yet ease hearts and consciousness,
from whose corners and variety
a marvellous pleasure might arise,
shall the roots of tenderness
in what we build and join and bless,
human city, shrivel – shall London
refuse her children part or portion?

Rosebay willow herb first invaded
this ugly dereliction,
left to rot and trap unheeded,
sacred malediction –
already one child sacrifice,
to what horrendous god?
We can no longer let this property
breed destruction.
New generation make free
of your bit of London.

The second invasion, of children,
was not mournful like the weed.
Like active goats they press in cheerfully.
Wilful for survival
on stubborn urban soil,
they lug and tug loads
to make it good.

They interrupted us with bulldozers.
('The site is earmarked
for a carpark.' Why and when?)
This is the machinery
of government smashing us down,
those meant to be,
by our appointment,
servants, turned dragon.
Shall the iron caterpillars
of unreason
still undermine our struggling cures,
crush future women?
Weep but return, single-minded,
till conceded the land is ours,
for a season – playspace – we won.

COME BACK

Sometimes when I find you gone,
I cannot cope with my despair.
How many miles to Babylon?
I have no transport here.
Poem come back again.
I ask no supernatural aid.
I do not trust the works of God.
Only your proper motion
to carry me thither.
For with no wordpower in my body,
when beauty chokes me,
I am worse than alone,
there is no self there.
Poem come back again,
you are mine, you are me.
Bring viewless wings or a hoverplane,
but to grin from the belfry
is more than unfair
when I rot in the desert of Araby.
It is murder.

And thus I watch my infant sleep
whose quietness makes me distrustful.
How can a person fall so deep
and respiration be so still.
Child come back again.
I shake it awake unkindly,
consoled and frightened by the cry.
Sometimes when I hear her weep
I could smother and kill

to put us both out of our misery,
but my hands more prosily
steadily rock to keep
wailer and me from evil.
Child come back again.
Let us be happy,
now try your wonky smile newborn.
Now let me let you be
in my muddle.
Since you are life to me,
I become gentle.

And thus from mutual banishment
we want to return together.
How to get over resentment?
Can we if we care?
Love come back again.
I am clumsy and sore
and you are touchier than before.
But your shoulders are bent
as they always were
and your shoulder blades move deliciously.
You mutter to me
with some bewilderment
and stroke my hair.
Love come back again,
you are necessary.
Absence and silence
defences are broken
now that we see each other,
and when we fall freely
we get there.

BODY OF WORK

Poetry is of the body,
hence its difficulty. Statistics are unable
to predict its mean absence
or make provision for truancy.
The wretched creature is free
and incalculable.
Music's a stubborn mule
and words fall dead when overloaded
by my hustling greed.
To market, to market!
Get out of the cart you idle animal!
But Brown Bear will not dance
for Master Clown in melancholy
or if his furry limbs
are sluggard at breakfast time.

Poetry is about the body,
an accurate agony of respected detail.
It must love the human face,
get right more than its beauty;
an abstract is a mockery
of the embattled personal.
A poet to be truthful
must not boss but have understood,
to do must have endured.
Get it out, get it out.
So be affectionate, be very humble.
Your voice's grace convinces
by attending to the workaday
of common planted word; its stress,
pitch, tone, tune: the marvellous rose.

O SAPIENTIA

O Wisdom sounded from the mouth of the Most High,
resounding from end to end, to care for all things
strongly and sweetly, come and teach us carefulness.
Magnificat Antiphon for 17th December

1

'I got the Knowledge
on Thursday.' Dear God I thought
not dear old Reg
a goner to the Guru,
that great con,
false righteousness, erasure
of the tender young uncertain
what on earth to do.

I remembered Cath,
how her mind was sharp and bright,
always a good laugh
we had, till she became
bored by troubles,
blank at an idea, desire,
even people's looks and details
passed with that null beam.

Reg takes a medallion
out of his left breast pocket,
not religious coin,
but heart's delight, a licence
for a cab.
London learnt is skilful pleasure –
back street, cinema, pub, kerb,
saving your presence.

59

2

'She's proud,'
said the carpenter.
'Plane 'er more.'
Curls were shaven,
then he stroked
her smoothed side,
now a perfect fit
for closure,
a working door.

'You lead your LCC
into your threeway
saltglaze spigot,'
said the plumber.
He showed his little lad
what earth to scoop out
in the small yard,
set in the sculpture
and made the
connection.

I praised
the particular word,
used in the trade.
I praised the lordliness
of men who demanded
a daily lorry-load
of clinker
so that tradesmen
should not walk in mud.

I praised exactitude
in a skill.
For the saving word
must be set
in the earth
like the spigot,
patted and humbled
her breadth,
like the door's pride.

Adherents of the Guru Mahara-ji refer to their conversion as getting the Knowledge. The exam that London taxi drivers have to pass is also called the Knowledge.
    A door or window is called proud when it jams in its frame. LCC is 2 inch pipe.

HOODS

Motherhood
covered the body,
muffled its free speed,
discovered the mind
it now inhabited
multitudinous consciously.
The child is my own kind.
I am bewildered
by her loveliness,
minutely detailed girl.
Under her scrutiny
I cry, kindness find,
hold her till the need
is over. She goes
when she's grown. Rejoice.
Let not the cowl
cover a body
old with envy,
discover a mind
cold with greed.

Childhood
ran bareheaded,
one day locked
the grown up people
in their greenhouse,
watched their furious
mouthings among the tomatoes
and laughed rolling in mud,
proved her small country
stone by roofing stone

for woodlouse and unknown insect,
periwinkle, badger hole,
and through it tracked
her secrecy.
I am five and alive
and unless I die,
which I won't just yet,
no one can stop me,
and just you wait,
you will *lionise* me.

Casting down their golden crowns
around the glassy sea,
in the end shall they be
as they were in the beginning –
without bonnet my mother bore me?
In between tried many hoods,
some fitted for achieving
chosen goods, some foisted on,
some hid corruption or empty heads,
but should they stand in flesh on the new earth –
and the sheer acoustics
of that unshaped hope are found
in most of us, somewhere beneath
getting and spending
and that free commonwealth
has already begun
in small ways and unlikely places,
just as children playing naked prophesy –
that day they won't stand ignorant.
Bared heads are risky and the politics
of innocence an achievement.

THE DEATH OF ALLENDE

Did the gentle Allende
sit down on the sofa in his palace
and shoot himself in the mouth
with the rifle given him
by his friend?
The bombs were falling
and the bulls came in.
At evening
they carried out his body
and the general bulls,
as reasonable soldiers
with democracy
and a constitution to defend
suspended congress.

Blood in the streets of Santiago.
I don't want to see it.
Their president duly elected
gave all he had
did what he could
to spare it.
To stop a tank, he said,
how many masses?
He didn't want to see the blood.
Blood in the streets of the city
and in the ITT hotel,
champagne cheers
to the military radio,
crocodile tears.

You were the hero,
Salvador Allende,
who tried the hardest road
to bring the common good
and life abundantly
upon your earth,
restore it
to its workers
so that they might not
go hungry
to profit
their masters.
But in three short years
that wasn't easy.

From the jaws of the jackals
in criminal North America,
you wrested the minerals,
claimed the copper,
rightfully your people's,
yes, rightfully yours.
Milk you provided
for Chile's children.
Even this first need
the Moloch of mammon
had denied, ignored starvation.
You tried for the necessary
schools and doctors,
roads and other lifegivers.

And in Washington they determined
your downfall
from the beginning.
And at home the princes plotted
with the bulls
to see your ending.
Now they silence your defence,
burn books
and Pablo Neruda is dead.
Murder and torture
are the norm of their beastly rule
and Allende your failure
disgraces us all
who gave no assistance.

You were that rational star
of necessary innocence
to seek first justice
and kind godless sense,
but the sleek boot
soon put a stop to that
and the goosestep on your human face.
You died but did not surrender,
Salvador Allende
badly needed
as the dew, the rain,
and as the earth is broken open
by green things pushing in spring,
you should have succeeded.

1973

66

PREPOSITIONS AND
CONJUNCTIONS
1977

WITH IT

Ever so Zeitgeist

I'm free
to dispose of myself
creatively
in the novel womanpattern.
Look at me –
not on the shelf
(superceded conceptualisation) –
I elect a viable container,
squat to achieve closure
towards the realised eschatology
of the day of the dustman.

THROUGH

A tidy life,
dreams filed
sensibly away,
a work routine . . .
you are OK.

Kiss the impossible
foreigner, joke
figure of a
Latin lover
for light relief.

It wasn't the bedbliss
that did it
but the shock
of the person
also naked,
ridiculously exotic,
unexpectedly lovable.

Conversation rooted
tapped deep down
a welling tenderness.
Passion didn't wither
but sprang to a strong tree
where the wild birds could nest.

Total upheaval,
self loss,
glorious irresistible
woozy surrender
among the other,
manic expanded mutual
consciousness.

Open: vulnerable –
depression of huge hurt
in the process
of knowledge increasing,
in the necessary
daring to reassert
self naturally.

Slash the symbiotic
doom of less than one,
disperse the solipsistic
fog of fantasy.

Under the winter sun
at the solstice
the earth is alive.
We believe the growth.

AWAY

A Sicilian Mother's Lament

I never thought
he'd go so far away,
my son, I loved him so.
Even when he was small
he was so dependable:
he mended the television,
he unstopped the drain,
he fixed the electricity,
he drove the car
far better than his father,
went shopping with me –
such an eye he had
for choosing my dress material.
He was always clever
and so beautiful.

I watched his career
through school and university,
the chance we'd never had.
When he got his degree
in Biological Sciences,
his Uncle offered to buy him
a private laboratory.
He wouldn't have it, although
he'd have been comfortably
settled and still in Palermo.
But no – he went to London.

'Mamma I'd suffocate
in this city.
Let me free.
Let me go it
alone.'

I never thought
you'd be
so far away
my son.

So now he's gone.
What should I do
for the rest of my life
with my children grown?
They were my all.
I gave my soul.
I find no residue.
Round and round the family we go,
polite in the long afternoon
and they pity me now
for my longing, degraded
from strong motherhood,
still young enough
but no longer needed.
I am dry inside.

Her heart is a broken
abandoned Fiat.
Hot scrap metal
knifes tender feet
on the coast of a world's cradle,
polluted Mediterranean.

An infernal wind
whips the unfriendly sand,
her little one's playground.
The sea is still cool blue.
Her eyes are blind.

And the still small voice
whispers selflessness
is the sin against the spirit
never forgiven.

Did you intend this,
my God, my Son?

BACK TO

Stepmother

Me she hated
without rhyme or reason.
She wedded my dad
when I was ten.
I couldn't win.
Nothing I did
altered
her goddess condemnation.
In painful fear
I avoided her,
responded
with hate I hid.

Now I know
she's a parasitical,
cruel illiterate.
At thirty-four I still
redden and tremble,
back in that state,
reverberate:
Bad and small,
when I telephone
my father and 'Her again,'
she whinnies down the hall,
'that loopy gal.'

EITHER OR

Had Both Ways

It is hard to endure the loneliness
of having no one
familiar at home to share with.

It is hard to endure the frustration
of the compromise
made with whoever you live with.

It is hard to bear childlessness,
cut off from delicious bodies
in their time of most startling growth.

It is hard to put up with children,
tedious and relentless,
exhausting and uncouth.

We become acquainted with death
and loathe it both
in maroon isolation
and chocolate togetherness.

OUTSIDE

Exilé sur le sol au milieu des huées,
ses ailes de géant l'empêchent de marcher.
                  BAUDELAIRE, *L'Albatros*

(Stuck on the ground, pelted abuse,
his giant wings are a fat lot of use.)

As a child I enjoyed riding,
jogged to a knowledge of the country.
I preferred to ride alone,
smell the sap of advancing bracken
and sandy floored resinous pines,
plunge down combes to streams
in the scrub oak valleys –
water curling over lucent stones,
twisted diminished trees hardily
clinging to acute angles my pony
braved like a wise toboggan.
I loved a springy heather cradle
or sheep-shorn soft turf to lie on
and be filled with sky.
But I did not feel comfortable
at home, or get on at all
as I grew up in county society.
I felt wrong and did not belong.

I started praying, loudly turned RC
but the Church with its foreign pomps
and the Pope with his golden phone
never felt ordinary – too bossy.
I preferred to pray alone,
the liturgical romps
were a Latin thrill, emotional antics
with passionate friends, communion
a savagely private act by me.
I wasn't much good at community.
I joined in marxist politics.
Their bossiness was worse.
I offered myself for an equality
apparently mainly for men.
I tried to force myself to use
their queer English but couldn't check
the wicked laughter bubbling from deep down.
I felt wrong and did not belong.

Though I listen with admiration
to every variety of my mother tongue,
I remain an outsider
from 'popular culture'.
I quickly feel bleak and uneasy
with lacked conversation at meal times,
fussing round the food and programmes
for the rest of the night on television.

I hate housework, aim at a minimum,
not a devoted career.
Bustling round the male
to background musack makes me suicidal.
I'm stuck up but I've kept my song.
I'm idle but do esteem people,
especially vigorous women pressing
for social change with splendid energy,
whether essential or a detail,
but I feel wrong and do not belong.

Still I find the albatross
silly to boast,
more of a waste really.
In a just republic
more perhaps most
would be poets.
If it cast them out
it would end up empty,
so there each could wish
for a niche.

WITHOUT

Sans Peur et sans Reproche

Don't most people think of poetry
as a heavy frivolity,
a no longer entertaining
intractable penny-farthing?
Who cares if clowns fall
yet again? The joke's over.
Neither is it a respectable
vehicle for an idea.

A straightforward novel
with a proper story
is so much more enjoyable.
You can slump in cosily,
really get to know the people
this winter night, and feel less lonely.
Poetry is not a good read:
it is often short, irritating and hard.

Poetry does not sell
so why do we do it?
Poets are problematic and marginal
to the economy. Their ends meet
seldom, their children 'insecure'.
They fussily tinker and fumble
over precarious livings compatible
with: I must write: I must recite.

We do it for pleasure.
The sharp gasp of the heart
at chaos caught and harnessed:
that's it, precisely, yes!
the longing, the tingle, the silkiness
of the body of the language beast:
O lovely animal of sound at one
with the irreproachable precision.

So Bayard *sans peur*,
our unoriginal schoolgirl idol,
do you reappear
caparisoned thus
from that distant past,
and you crude images of puberty
were fodder and pressure of poetry?

For also in the ordinariness
of our dear English
don't we find relish and solace?
Millions speak it
for whom learning it was childsplay,
a very cheering thought.
The poet edges in attentively,
loves, listens, burns
with common verbs and nouns.

WITHIN

On Looking at a Spanish Mat

Lipizaner sleek closed pattern,
double perfection
of shape and colour
recommending each other –
crimson to pink on elephant brown,
leafy cross, full moon,
symmetrical tadpole squiggles

within twin opposite
pairs of bracket curls,
a horizontal short and fat
exactly half the size
of the slenderer vertical –
hypnotically satisfies
but cruelly may imprison.

Since when you break out
it breaks down,
if you don't want that
you have to wait until
the glorious, anarchical
annunciatory light breaks in,
flows to metamorphose your vision,
softly fills your eyes.

IN

I am my body
subject to irritability.
In a bleak mood
poetry seems an unlikely
and insubstantial good.
I cannot remember
the feel of the feeling of pleasure.
I cannot believe
a future might improve.

But joy slips in again
like a guerrilla unit
in a nocturnal takeover,
consolidates its power at daybreak,
normalising the situation,
so that I have forgotten
the dull pain dark.
Poetry now seems a naturally
appropriate action.

I am my body
and have to live
with a bloody succession
of negative and positive.
I age and alter but my mirror
is a certain continuity.
The rest is now outside me:
my large children won't fit back in
or the things I have written.

LOVE IN TIME
1982

LONDON

The fields from Islington to Marybone,
to Primrose Hill and St John's Wood
were builded over with pillars of gold
and there Jerusalem's pillars stood . . .
Pancras and Kentish Town repose . . .

                              BLAKE, *Jerusalem*

A damp chill lay upon London,
ordaining the rule of fear:
grab what you can,
stockpile security,
property, food, weapon,
hit first, beat your neighbour,
snap up, become gross,
for you are utterly alone
and times are lean.

A damp chill lay upon London,
ordaining the worship of force
as the desirable, so-called masculine:
thrust yourself, be brutal,
bully, hurt and abandon
the distressed, the vulnerable
who take care of the children.
Every meanness, every evasion
will cnsure you get on.

A damp chill lay upon London,
ordaining the groan of the people
while directors gorged in the Hilton.
The smug rulers were cynical and snug
amid dereliction.
Twenty pounds was the dole
of over three million.
Bracing lies were spoken
while our wills were broken.

This chill mist, a philosophy
of necessary hierarchy,
appealed to greed regarded
as the evil human core,
which is not true.
Still the spirit blew.
Well, I'll be blowed
and in the river wisdom flowed.
Government's fall is only the small start
of survival. We must part
with the dominative-servile mode.
Life sprouts everywhere
even in this bleak air.

This is the London I love,
where hosts of poets speak
in spite of the impeding medium
in which they swim,
seek to utter their city
and redeem it. The dance goes on
to jazz and reggae time.
Arm in arm the young girls
walk in beauty, moonlit,
dove-tender, spunky-smart:
'Fuck the dole, we'll have a laugh!'
And with luck young men are gentler,
less snarled up, in this generation.

Here when with broken heart
I prowled the streets to howl
at dead of night –
don't frighten children sleeping –
a milkman counsels, 'Cheer up duck,
if he's no good why worry?
Tell him where he gets off
and find a better one.
Show some bottle girl.'

He hands me into his lorry,
stops at the doss house to buy me Weights
from the ancient machine
and drives me home.
'Milk. Here take it.
Make yourself a nice cuppa tea,
then get tucked up quick. You're welcome.'
And leaves me safe
with perfect courtesy.

Here you can go for a paper
in gumboots and nightgown
and Mr Patel in the shop says, 'Good morning,'
and rounding the corner
the socialist postman.
Here you can break the stranglehold
of the conventional mould,
live, love as you please, make new,
and the large tolerance of the city
will leave you be.
And if you crash and feel a fool,
it will not be forever.
London soothes and still enfolds you.

Familiar village, urban abandon
and the street sagas on they go.
Eccentricity, passion and high courage.
Bridie generous, poor and tough,
her fifth (German measles) born deaf
got into the leatherwork college.
Henry spent Christmas mending his car
flat on his back in inches of snow.
Operatic in the midnight street,
four-leafed mother, the red-haired Maureen
gets shut of her boring, bruising man,
sings: 'I don't love you any more,'
and dives for cover next door.

Even the stiff-permed peeping moaner
is allowed her character:
'Such goings-on at number eight!'
And on New Year's Eve the buses shudder
with rude and cheerful song.
London has seen it all.
London has suffered long.
This is a kind and patient people,
who also speak with tongues of men and angels.

Still the spirit blew.
Well, let's be blowed
and in the river wisdom flowed.
Rulers have got it wrong
to underestimate this yeasty dough,
such excellent ingredients.
How long till this people rises
against their insolence?
People of London, how long?

And come the resurrection,
laugh my dears. You have the right
to rejoice and be glad.
For haven't you escaped
the devil's toils
and broken the strong chain
that bound you all those years.
Life sprouts everywhere,
even in this bleak air.

1981

91 .

AGAINST FALSE PROFITS

The one day
the predator
no longer thrilled the prey,
cruelty chilled,
masochism palled.
Now at last the dominator
gasped for love and met rebuff:
That's enough!
Killed I still
call your bluff.
Thus you are my enemy,
my heart won't play.

The evening star
rose over the undergrowth
tangling the forest floor
and every night creature
awoke to its work,
pressing and pulsing,
creeping and crawling,
hunting and hiding.
Our kind has a mind that's freer
but we are unkind to each other,
we don't restore what we take,
our weapons threaten the earth.

The slick cosmopolitan
Me generation
is a sick Yank joke.
Nietzsche's superman
is a dangerous pain.
I speak and listen
carefully to your answer
because we seek.
Otherwise we are barbaric
with our mod cons
and dizzy high tech,

arrogant schizoid science
demanding obeisance
(and money) withdrawn
from ordinary care
of actual people,
the political will
to make sense as a whole.
Knowledge is priestly power.
Distinction of good and evil
is heresy in the laboratory
or just an embarrassing bore.

The selfish gene
against its own species
masquerades as a justification
of those ladies with dominant hats
and screeching voices.

To raucous cries of: Sin!
(Disgusted Surbiton),
National Service! (Pow!)
Bring back the cane! (Ow!)
Compete, damn you, it's a race! –
fumbling together somehow
we embrace, become human.

Venus' modest light
angel of the glory of clear night
attracts our eyes.
Inkling insight,
oh but heartsease:
Shine gratis.
Grace abounding
shames the market place,
for the ungenerous
is the ultimate loser
and the first, worst death
is unrisked mutuality.

Stronger and weaker,
this kills both,
quoth she.

EXMOOR REVISITED

ALLERFORD

Here the main weather is rain
and the vegetation is outrageous,
huge and multifariously green,
lush grass, giant rhubarb,
runner beans, lusty shrubs
of rose of Sharon,
fuchsias triple the London size,
placid enormous trees outspread
in idiosyncratic satisfaction
against the active sky.
Everything grows and blows,
struggles ruggedly on
and every awaited harvest
is threatened by tempest.

This was the country
that mothered my imagination
but later the fact still shocked
that human birth and making
also needed and could summon
such patience and such energy.
The sun is never more numinous
than here when it glistens after rain.

HORNER WATER

I rode here,
a child promoted
to my first horse
with some breeding and speed.
Along the deep valley bottom
we twist with the rushing stream
adazzle under the sunned
precipitous scrub oak,
transfigured green gleam.
I loved the red earth and stone.

High up on top
heather on Dunkery
and the sky
was azure of peace
and longing between rain.
Muscle of eager gentle animal,
movement, heart, nature,
contented self yet trusting
an expected unknown future
to work a miracle.

Away from stepmum
grim ruled home,
I am happy alone today
believing somewhere out there
the saviour is he
who will see and approve,
redeem me, offload
the burden of solitude.
This welcome and appalling
half life was called love.

Though the silk of faith
was shot subversively
with selfhood's healthy sheen,
those times of deep vision
when the whole being restfully
enjoys what it is
were devalued provisional,
especially for women,
unless seen and fulfilled
by god or some other male.

Here I return twenty years after
with grown children
ahead up the hill –
love and let go, don't cling,
pray nothing much goes wrong.
But having also loved excessively
the craved-for saviour figure
in many guises – just let him move well
as that pony, pubertal measure still
of the beautiful and strong,

I've been wounded, abandoned.
Now the green heals me
and the clatter of water
and whooshing of trees.
I am glad of the power to love exceedingly,
thankful for love I've been given.
But today as the sun
bursts through cloud and enlightens,
I feel whole and in patience
I possess my soul.

GIRL THIRTEEN

Three friendly cats
attend her
as she fiercely
at thirteen
struggles to womanhood,
coming from junior calm,
appalled at the primal scream
of adult sexuality.

Really it's ludicrous
that mother
at her age
should still indulge
a demon lover,
be all smiles and kisses
on Saturday night,
dawn Monday animal rage
howling down the house.

She the daughter
curls on a large red cushion,
graceful honeysuckle sprawl.
Two black cats stroll proud.
Tabby furrily tucked close
purrs soporifical,
stroked with love,
as the troubled poppy head
stoops over in repose.

Tiger lily straight
she walks and does not
permit interference.
Her joy distils cartwheels,
sister still to Catherine martyr.
The articulate cruelty
of her rudeness stuns.
Her superb sulks jelly them all.
She absolutely appeals.

MAPPING

HEDGE

She is so busy,
nurturing,
clearing their way,
refuelling them.

When she is lazy,
anxieties nudge.
She is the drudge
of habit,

clinging,
self–emptying,
cannot stop it,
even when one day
busy is busybody,

because low esteem
has forced her poem
out to the edge
to consort with poppy
and the weed herb robert.

But if she can trudge
up the courage
to get there and sit,
the field is clearly
defined by the hedge.

RIDGE

The final grapple
up to this high ledge
was sheer black rock,
granite sliced vertical –
no footholds. I floundered
and backslid into the bramble
from which I strove to emerge.
I am all scratched
and stained purple.

I have reached it
the ridge, the open,
wide turf track braids it,
then curves, dips down the new side.
Safely sheep graze.
At this stage I'm on velvet.
I look backwards
over the steep wooded country
I came from, to nursery slopes.

For a while I walk level.
So this is the top of the hill,
the view both ways.
Enjoy it I will,
till the drop
to the next opaque thicket,
the eventual stop.

LOVE IN TIME

TO A LADY IN A SONNET

Dalek Petrarch

You silent lady, who manipulate
and are degraded to a fantasy,
we wanted neither, would not tolerate
those schizoid blokes, more perfect ecstasy
to overcome the split, both care and speak,
and share the ancient knowledge with our men.
Aghast they either grovelled and felt weak
or machoed smartly back to their machine.
Platonic hierarchies that hate the earth:
a monster now equipped for genocide.
A hideous contract brings no saving birth:
risk passion dangerous on Beachy Head.
Trapped lady, will your daughters, once naive
now battered, terminate or reconceive?

ISOLATION

This aching shock ticks bitter loneliness,
whose bloodless lessening thuds dead unrest
excruciating language bodiless,
frustration sickens at the wicked waste.
I cannot love unless in solitude
I am my own and by myself enjoy
my proper work, sweet idleness, good food
and feel at ease in my own company.
False selflessness, a heavy breathing stone,
deep drowns the other even with goodwill.
Virtue stands in curious admiration,
kneels slave to no man, gives with grace and skill.
The dark night either teaches and restores
another day, or we become its jaws.

CONFESSION

I am not under any other law
but this: to love and then do as I will.
My soul is glad: the idol rules no more,
although the violent dead still try to kill.
Free now to recreate love every day,
the trouble is we are responsible
for when we make mistakes, and we must pay
by knowing we have hurt when we meant well.
I'm sorry for the damage I have done,
ashamed and chastened by the muddled mess
of feckless selfishness, inflicted pain,
especially when children paid the price.
Still, I had rather fail, repent, forgive
and stagger on, than be afraid to live.

IN PERFECT TIME

This is the point when we are innocent,
we strip and join at once each time we meet
and bring together every element:
unfallen angels don't have such delight.
The love that moves the sun and other stars,
mute weight of every creature's urgent day,
here reaches speech and at our coming cheers:
poles hold and fold the world, its core this joy.
All well. But we are animals of earth
whose pulse dictates that static union
is bliss but brief or death. Life must be growth;
kindness can't prevent that separation.
Those who have sometimes tasted paradise
escape, through hope, the pit of bitterness.

MOTHER TO SON

How short a time ago you were distressed
and cried when you surprised our noise in bed.
I could not touch you, could not give you rest,
pubescent, spotty, judging, full of dread.
Enormous eyes of lion-lamb appear,
you bring her shining in to breakfast noon.
We smile when Mary wants to cut your hair,
the women, while you shrug and bask in sun.
My youth collapses, I have bred a man,
bonfire salutes superb and fragile bliss.
You pat me kindly, now of course you can
forgive, and turn to give your girl a kiss.
This reconciliation lets love know
it's time to shove again, soon you must go.

TO MY CAMDEN POETRY GROUP

Yes, I am nasty, I admit you're right,
I get bad tempered at poor quality,
I hurt when I'm impatient for delight,
please take account of human frailty.
But now that powers of darkness threaten doom,
let me salute each individual voice
stuttering for utterance in this tatty room:
we are the living, come let us rejoice.
For if this Christmas here a child is born
in bare simplicity, its name is Hope,
who will have many mothers, not just one
madonna, fathers too, since god can't cope.
We are, we make the word and hence may love;
there is no other trinity above.

CHORUS

Now suddenly our time on earth seems short,
another London spring excites the air.
Street children gallop on the grass and shout,
trust thrusting freer from their mothers' care.
A blessing on fresh couples in the park,
unconquered sun strokes even stiff old bones.
Joy stirs, disturbs once more before the dark:
I am it all, heart hurts, sheer pleasure groans.
The utterable ground of love is this:
it matters how we are and what we do,
adore all flesh knowing all flesh is grass,
the mystery is you; and you; and you.
Quick quality of detail is the thing
that marks the common time in which we sing.

GLAD RAGS
1983/4

GLAD RAGS

Now the negative forces are clever and bold
flaunting their victory for all to behold.
They appeal to the worst in us, hate, fear and greed
and the state of this country is bitter indeed.

We are poor, we are anxious, lethargic and ill.
If we eat or keep warm, we can't pay the bill.
'You wicked old woman!' authorities cry,
'to fall into debt: why not starve, freeze and die?'

And parents see children lose hope and lose heart,
when at last they leave school and are ready to start
and nobody wanting their strength and their skill
and everything crumbles including their will.

And the rich are entrenched and they don't give a damn.
They have the bread as well as the jam.
'Kick whiners and scroungers – it's jolly good sport.
We've got the Old Bill, the army and jolly good port!'

Friends, we are at a loss
and hope is failing.
Now is the hour of Grendel
and our hall is frail.
He is prowling outside,
softly he treads, pad, pad.
His howling invokes unreason,
calls upon chaos
appalling to break in.
It is the crunch of the truncheon.
It is the moan of the missile.
Friends, we are not well
and night is falling.

'It is better to struggle
than greatly mourn.
Life in this world
is a short term
for each one of us.
Let us resist evil,
act while we can,
speak and leave a name.'

'Dance!' sneered the Nazi soldier
to the stripped gipsy
in the queue to the gas chamber.
For she had been a superlative dancer.
So she did.
And was at once restored
to life and pride.
She seized his revolver
and managed to shoot a guard
before they got her.

In the jaws of death,
in the mouth of hell,
dance defiance to destruction.
She danced well.
But until doom is certain,
hope still and you shall sing
a possible change of heart
and transformed city.
Poet, keep faith with humanity.
Let your poem excel:
it is your clear duty.
Eschew rubbish, Tories, narcissists,
Martians, gurus, pseudo-mystic quietists.

Then you are free to interpret
that strange lightness of spirit
that sprouting of new spring
shown in friendship, belief,
achievement in common
or when alone not for private profit
but offered, taken, made part,
the relief and joyful quality
of altered lives,
whose social new creation
solves the riddle of simplicity.

This revolution is our festival –
for yes, we are oppressed.
Let each hint and moment of it tell
of the greatly desired rest.
It is not too late.
Put on your glad rags,
don't sag, be brave-voiced,
save hope, celebrate.

ON MY WAY

Going not long ago
to a gig at Dalston Junction,
all dressed up in my poetry kit,
glitter and tat,
under the wide twilight
on Camden Road Station
I strode reciting my lines,
the bits I might forget.

To summon the right spirit,
I conjure the evening star:
O Venus O
goddess, I cry to her,
let the duende
possess me tonight.

Three lads and I get into the train.
'You going a party?' asks one.
'No,' I reply, 'I'm a poet.'
'Yer what?
I thought you was a nutter.'
'No,' I say, 'I'm not.
Not a nutter but a poet.'
'Oh yer. I bet.
I bet you never
rhymed two words togever.'
'Oh Gaw!' I hear the other mutter,
'perhaps you are an' aw.'

I see him stare at me
with fascinated horror
in case I break out,
have a queer turn and shout.
They hastily alight at Highbury.
'Goodnight,' now nervous and polite.

LUST

On the piano, your hands,
broad flat nails, quick fingers.
Your shoulders hunched over.
Sweet neck, that singing throat.
Thick Greek belt, your walk:
yes, you can move all right.
(Call this a raid on the inarticulate?)

I don't understand those women
who demand disgust
in outraged arguments against penetration,
who make daisy chains to deck
a sister's correct political gesture,
who tick me off for craving impossible men.
(OK. We pay,
I agree, but couldn't we
change that a bit?)
In love, in lust
I like a proper fuck.

Only the violence of eros
conquers the violence of death,
thanatos, mighty conflictors.
Life on earth, power of poetry
springs from the same force
as this painful awareness,
breathless pleasure in your body.
I don't want to hang or flog anyone
or sink the Belgrano.
I'd rather lie with you all afternoon.
But he played the piano.

DEVICES AND DESIRES

It won't be them
who press the button
to release the bomb
but us.

Yes we condemn
the faceless bosses
who control the bomb
but we are like them,
we indulge the same weakness,
commit the same sin.
They have human hearts
and names like us.

We have followed too much
the devices and desires
of our own hearts.
We have left undone those things
we ought to have done
and done those things
we ought not to have done.

It won't be him
who sends the flame deluge
to end the world
but us.

In my violent rage
I have shaken small children –
brats whining for sweets –
screamed abuse at innocent typists,
felt my hands tingle
with the thrilling desire
to throttle my adversary,
barely quelled
an insistent urge to burn down
the Circolo Gramsci club in Dean Street,
because I loved and had quarrelled
with one Italian.

A flash of rage:
'Let 'em have it!'
may give the order
to send the bomb,
a flash of rage
as common and no greater
than I have felt often
and I'm sure that you
have experienced too.

It won't be them
who press the button
to release the bomb
but us.

In a fit of greed,
neurotic, fattening need,
I have crept out alone to the baker,
bought myself a whole apple pie
and stuffed it
where no one could see,
not wanting to share it.
I have hidden wine
when I heard the doorbell
and once became hysterical
when someone took a book of mine
and lent it at work
and for months was too shy
to ask for it back.
I did not want to read it then,
merely to secure possession.

A fit of greed:
'I want it!'
may give the order
to send the bomb,
a fit of greed
as common and no greater
than I have felt often
and I'm sure that you
have experienced too.

It won't be them
who press the button
to release the bomb
but us.

Despair is the mortal sin,
when the owl hoots in the dark night
and you mope too and try to cry
but your heart's so tight, your soul so dry,
only a drop of bile oozes out.
You cower under fetid covers
(the washing machine of course is broken),
desire nothing, no touch, no sound,
you are bruised fruit all over,
scratchy as sand on the beach
by the town tip for shattered idols,
where family saloon, colour telly,
faithless hi-fi lie abandoned
among the rats and dead cats
of your Mediterranean holiday.
You just wish the world would go away.

Inertia won't lift a finger
to stop it, lets anything happen.
Despair doesn't care anymore
who presses what button
anywhere. It wants nowhere.
The bomb may occur
as a longing for non-being,
surrender to total failure.
Despair is the great sin, the fatal
temptation assailing us all.

*It won't be him
who sends the flame deluge
to end the world
but us.*

This time there may be no ark,
even under High Wycombe car park.
No, Noah, nowhere to go.
This fire
licks up the rainbow
like a fuse wire.

LIFE AGAINST DEATH

Sunday December 12th 1982

All day within the enclosure
of Greenham Common,
the military busily
whizzed up and down
in sinister looking vehicles,
dark anonymous trucks
buzzing along the tarmac
for no clear reason,
maybe containing uneasy personnel
protecting themselves from the women –
who rise like lions after slumber
distinctly in disturbing number,
anarchic and wholly at one –
maybe in routine treks
or checks of their tophole work
to welcome the missiles,
the mightiest mock pricks
this world has ever seen,
no semen but seeds of destruction,
whose sorrowful journey
is speedy doomsday.

We held hands in a nine mile circle
round the perimeter fence,
which we had brought to life
by love and common sense
with grass-woven symbols,
messages, teddy bears, balloons,
woollen webs, roses, babygrows,
knitted bootees, poems, photos,
paper christmas trees with streamers,
many banners as the morning rising
(who is she? – Wisdom), Dutch, Norwegian,
solemn compound German from the Greens.
We planted primulas still flowering
and snowdrop bulbs in hope.
We sent round kisses and apples of peace,
hand to hand, face to face.
There was singing, dancing, picnicking –
soggy sandwiches, brandy, oxtail soup.
And the spirit was like a mountain,
old and strong.
It was a sturdy, cheerful quickening.

CAMDEN TOWN GARDEN

Neat, rigid, bleak, pounded,
how you humbled and hounded me hard
with your huge heavy hammer strokes,
dull thud, dull thud, you thunder
on the thick concrete oblong slab
along the shabby house front,
ontological gap between lodging and pavement.
Strong arm rhythm, wrath
ruthless, relentlessly breaking off fragments.
Then the practised pick seeks
spreading cracks, presses under,
lifts, shifts, splits
brick-rooted continents presumed monolithic
and look, I am earth beneath.

Armour discarded, more soil added,
lightened and sweetened with peat,
wood ash scattered for good renewal,
the embedded bulb multitude
meekly in wicked winter waits.
How long it takes to be over,
sour survival day after day,
dark and apparently blank
dank patience, gruelling grey.
Nothing to do but get through it,
allow the invisible growth to occur,
submit to slow process, don't force it:
as space and peace for shoots to stir,
merely endure and be thankful.

But what if this winter wastes me away?
What if the bulbs are dud?
Or worst, the worn out year won't turn?
In language-lorn, bandaged January
shears the darkness, dares the air
miraculous crocus blade,
upright heroine, prim pioneer,
so slight for such salutation.
By late March the patch is a riot.
After the wait it is here,
spring sprung from previous concrete,
London clay that lay
bound down a hundred winters long.
Recovery is a new song.

LAW AND ORDER

1

It's Tory policy
to give these people
a short sharp shock:
jolly good idea!

Late again last week,
I biked through Regent's Park
against regulations.
As I approached the broad walk,
up roared a lorry,
abruptly braked by the fountain.
Two men jumped down,
walked round to the tackle at the back,
some crane-like ironmongery.

It's Tory policy
to give these people
a short sharp shock:
jolly good idea!

In a flash I knew
what they meant to do:
hang me,
string me high on that gibbet.
Well, I know Mrs Thatcher
wants to increase police power
but this is ridiculous,
summary execution
in Regent's Park of a poet
merely for riding a bike!

It's Tory policy
to give these people
a short sharp shock:
jolly good idea!

In the top gear of fear
I streaked across the bleak desert
of playing fields –
yes her jackals went to Eton –
I nearly had a heart attack
when I thought one bloke yelled:
'Oy, come back here!'
I ducked expecting the cackle
of machine gun fire.

Jolly good idea!

2

At the lorry's crackle on the gravel,
at the brake's squeal,
the cab door's slam,
men's menacing tread,
I had a clear perception,
I was certain:
this sequence is occurring
now at this minute
in El Salvador. My fright
is that felt by another
who is being hanged for real.
I could do nothing
but be with her in spirit.
I knew when she was dead.

Policy
to give these people
a short sharp shock.
Friends everywhere beware.

FOR NICARAGUA

Managua Nicaragua,
city with no centre
but the principle:
seek first justice.
We live on *gallo pinto*
and our dignity.

Now from the North
the Behemoth of Mammon,
Yankee rampant
Reagan the barbarian,
grins for his million fans
and threatens death.

They wickedly went out
to discredit your election
but you did not permit it.
Strictly to your honour
on this tricky occasion
it was conducted correctly.

And when sober witnesses
from Parliament in London
ate with two of your officials,
these mothers asked this favour:
If they invade and kill us,
take care of our children.

Admirable Nicaragua,
now your greatheart nutsweet
boys and girls stand fast
and seasoned older hands
are alert to defend you,
their rich and fruitful land,

from idolatrous murderers
who worship profit –
anything for a quick buck –
while you seek self rule,
instead of abject lack,
joy for your people.

You merely insist on justice,
thirst for peace.
We live on *gallo pinto*
and our dignity.
If they invade and kill us,
remember our children.

1984

Gallo pinto is a dish of rice and beans.

SOUL IN PARAPHRASE
1985

WOMAN IN A DRESSING GOWN

On the keen edge of morning
she does not dance,
no angel, more of a mist drifting.
In what sense does she exist?
A noise of passions ringing her for dead:
she can't get dressed.

She takes tea back to bed,
covets more rest.
Unshod, ungirded, unsafe fuzzy head,
she senses both at once
why Antony disarmed for dying,
Cleopatra dressed.

SOUL IN PARAPHRASE

DESIRE

Night after night
beached mer mammal,
kin to seal and dolphin,
she lies on her belly
and cries for the sea:
'Oh cover me, cover me,
my element, my delight.
Why do you never
kiss me under this moon?

I do not walk on knives
for an alien popinjay.
My pearly tail flaps,
I crave my salt love.
Oh cover me, cover me.
I am a large creature,
I am a load of desire,
unburden me of my sorrow.

My round breasts
press into the sand,
I scratch, I twitch, I am wet.
But my heart is parched,
I ache, am empty,
will you not fill me?
The crests of the waves are foamy,
he is strong and eager,
I hear him coming.

Oh reach me quickly.
do not abandon me
on this moon–bleached beach.
Dissolve me, cover me,
mighty lovable Neptune.
Hold me. Supple and light
I exult, I somersault.
Now take me. Take me now.'

DISAPPOINTMENT

I had to kill
the little sparrow
the cat got.
It quivered in pain
and would not fly again.

Summer of sour fruit,
summer of disappointment.
Unripened peaches split.
The mute and bitter serpent
slithers over the skin.

No post – bad morning –
stinging acrid sweat
brings out a rash of unfulfilment –
dead bees – sad pudding –
nipple prickles sing flat.

HAVOC

Unbreakable rock blocks the pass
unless the lever's pressed,
which springs it back
so that the Monstrous Murk escapes.

Freaks furious black unstoppable
recklessly wrecks wreaks
more damage than called for
darkroars till satisfied.

Then apologises,
slinks off sorry,
surprised that no one recognised
or named such common need.

Give me control of the lever,
words to conjure the animal:
O my rage, I hear you.
All will be well.
We shall overcome.
Lie down.

NERVE

Roof leaks, stop it with sticky tar,
thick and black like a babe's first shit.
Wall cracks, we imperfectly plaster it
with a slapped mixture of pinkish powder.
Light bulbs break, we are in the dark,
drains block and the sludge reeks of decay.
Propping and prodding keep the frail pad cosy
and fickly hold the primal soup in check.

Neither can we ban weakness from this bonehouse;
I bleed, I ache, I alter every day.
Skull lurks, disintegration stalks us,
I am unwomaned when I've had no tea.
I only find my centre now and then,
when good animal spirits give a shove
or where beyond tiredness joy slips in:
ocean, eros, here-earthly union, love.

And when I spin in centrifugal panic,
feel dizzy as the velvet night wears thin,
I do not flee the hound of heaven frantic
but from the hole I fear is where my centre should have been.
String snaps, I collapse, am disassembled.
How now scrap antiquated parts; add; see
whether this heap of heterogeneous junk all jumbled
fits back together another way?

Constantly. This is the price of every poem
and of living, every time it snarls up, wisdom.
The permanent point is cordial
being both membership and individual.
It needs a great heart not to deviate into religion,
courage to utter, endure chaos, utter anew,
nerve not to give up making and, with knots between,
thread the blood-red garnets, despite what death will do.

CONJUGATION

Singular and Plural

Now comes the hard grind
when violent passion
must gentle into patience,
possibly to no avail,
yet struggle to remain a loving soul.

Humble, singleminded.
That's it: purity of heart
is not to want one thing
but everything good, relate it –
at times this seems impossible –
in one vision with a single eye.
In order to become humble,
first a proper pride must be attained.

Anyway your true poet
does not harp but will respond
kindly to the whole
multiplicity of states of being
with a voice that is unmistakable.

PRAISE

'Praise, that's it!'
                    RILKE, *Orpheus Sonnets*

I praise sky,
not god for it, in it,
just itself this morning vast
fast variable sunfilled bowl,
where puffs float,
feathered streamers proceed,
high azure satisfies
a wide expanse of heath.

I praise heather,
not god for it, in it,
but its own intense colour,
light-crowned amethyst
peerless this year,
here on sloping sides,
hardly hills, lazy
all the way to the far wood.

I praise trees,
each one its own –
not god for it, in it –
shape, form, soul, material,
alive with secret growth,
praise be forever.
I come from the sun
to the cool of the forest beautiful.

Heather over there
extends to the sea,
steep cliff deep in bell and ling,
heathland to its last stand,
with fragrant bracken,
occasional gorse dazzle,
then smell of the sea, its sound.
Look down now and it fills the gaze.

And because here
the sea has so much weather,
may be but is not always
sweet speedwell,
also a luminous hazy silver,
outspoken indigo, alto violet,
sometimes storm black yellow,
in a climate moody but temperate,
I praise it for that.

Today it looks the colour of eyes
greenish greyish blue and mutable,
troubled when truth proves difficult
but whose smile is harebell
to cheat death of its sting.
I praise them too
and though I know no one is god
thankfully, I praise
you; and you; and you.

PEACE

Lovely curve of hill
is a mild ox resting at noon.
There at last sit still.
Empty tins that clattered in my head,
a mountain of litter discarded,
rag and bone man makes a killing.
Now a mild ox at noon,
I listen to the gorse pods popping.

On the train the sweetbriar brat
is a wild skilled irritation
to the dove-soft mother
drained dry grey with exhaustion.
The continual din persists
that whole wilderness-long journey.

The receptionist copy typist,
neat and clean through an exact discipline,
expertly flicks switches,
trying to connect you, simultaneously
types the curious prose –
she is scrupulous – of their busy effusions,
or tabulates sterling noughts.
She has sore eyes, a sick headache,
pulse ticks, successfully
polite all day, goes home a wreck.

And the glistering party girl
on a mega-rave, spinning, spinning.
Those decibels definitely deafen,
mum warns take care.

And in cornflower sunlight of huge desire
autumn touches the park.
Lads wheel barrows, Shakespeare knew them.
Greasy merchants on the pickup
stalk disconsolately unattractive.
Friends sit and talk.
Near the fountain where late roses bloom
a couple who now have made
just over a century between them
kiss and stroll on.

And let peace come
like cornflower sunlight on September trees,
like sweetness into fruit,
grass smell, warmth to the earth.
Let peace come,
noise cease for a little while,
listen with inward ear
now to the cordial voice,
listen well with imagination
to friends and all those strangers.

Peace possess all.
Let it steal onto your lap
like a favourite cat,
over your face like a smile,
catch you and hearten unawares
like a cheerful tune with rhythm.

Let peace come
to the party girl, the dove-soft mother
and the receptionist copy typist.
Listen to the gorse pods popping.

Be spared that other explosion.

TEA IN THE PARK

Thunder. Run for it?
Broken roses.
Acres of patient grass.
Weak tea for two
squashed under achieved roof.
Green rain on glass.
Eavesdropped explainings.
Acceptance, friendship, grief.

Lulled peace trip
to a secret wildgrown garden.
Trees drip. Wet underfoot.
Hives have bees.
Among small rocks she shows
prolific dark columbines,
white cotton stitchwort,
buttercups, poppies, herb robert.

TO A LATIN AMERICAN EXILE

Unlanguaged among strangers,
unbelonging in bleak sleeting rain,
you stand bewildered, travel-lorn
in a worrying, scurrying, foreign metropolis,
where their outlandish northern manners
chill your bones and blood,
are inscrutable barbarous codes,
even gestures minimal and mean.

Smug in their profitable ethic,
a nation of on-the-make traders,
quick with neat footwork to manipulate
and when the pubs open, alcoholic.
And where are the women? Horror!
These uncouth cannibal giantesses,
unfeminine, cold, lascivious,
might eat you quite without heart.

Please believe this frightful myth
is nightmare, not the full truth.

I know your homesickness, I feel your pain,
offer what I can to cure it.
At least I'll listen and translate.
I do love, do care, do mind,
and the first soil a shocked uprooted flower
will find to feed on is an indigenous friend,
then more, so may you not be rue
but heartsease, knitbone, feverfew.

For small herbs heal, flowers come, trees tower,
not just there, but here, on earth all over.

We are planetary citizens,
one sphere, one species,
and though the familiar loved particular
of word, sound, plant, food, custom, dress,
is birthright, sanity, hope of bliss,
poetry's ground to keep our feet on,
else the universal is an emptiness,
still there are human faces everywhere,
all detailed, some good, lovable too
once you get the habit.

Thus whether you stay or return,
may your rosemary of remembrance
bit by bit
become a less bitter brew.

COMING OUT OF IT

He did not really like the dark
but made it manfully,
like a child on a dare,
hurtling down the fearful corridor,
ghostly with ancestors,
to spit priestlike in the precious cup
and show them. Clitty naturally
might as well not have been there.
Afterwards a pulse ticked on his eyelid
and this, though obscurely unsatisfied
since she was not the object of desire,
she always loved him for.

And then the miracle:
the spittle was a little girl,
who smiled with his mild eyes,
grew like a happy lily,
perfect, a genetic masterpiece.
She was his joy,
his honey from rotten meat.
Out of the strong came forth sweetness:
'Oh, you're so strong!'
They always say that as they leave
and he left for a second mirror,
the hounding idea of the young hero.

ORPHEUS

Down he went down
to the dark to fetch her,
half his soul.
He failed to bring her back,
vocally besought fate
but to no avail.

She was already on the river
in the chilly boat.
'I am taken away
wrapped in enormous night . . . '
Then she faded like smoke
into air which is bodiless.

Without sap or any connection,
loose-leaf, feckless,
he drifted in manly mobility.
That kept dark and down
sprang as angry women
ripped him to pieces.

LOVE AND RAGE
1987

LOVE AND RAGE

Earful of sinuous rushing waters
thrash boulders veined ginger and cochineal,
fall, flash oak-filtered dragonfly lights.
Neat-footing banks nearly vertical,
eccentric joyous delicate deer
get away with it. In a lush clearing
seasparkle silky viridian grasses,
alluring an outbreak of utmost kisses,
then softness for earthbalm repose.

Let us go further into the thicket.
Sun disappears and the oaks close in.
The place of betrayal is mossy and damp,
near the source where by stout brambles
uncomfortable woody-stalked bilberries clump.
The trusted one, the beloved face
turned there, gored, drew blood and fled;
in panic withdrawal from the fearful dark
the bad friend shrank, ran out.

An animal in torment from jagged wound
roars with the burning of being abandoned.
In the unleashed storm trees crescendo
and swollen torrent descends in flood.
Till a pool from the spring stilled for a mirror.
Here rested the creature alone to recover.
And love was that spring with power to heal
whence, drumroll over, sang the stream
downvalley, uncoupled, to other people.

WHERE WAS I?

I am an unmapped country,
whose secret dark moors rove –
oh parabolas of purple heather
with your sweet summer smell! –
and forests far ungovernable
clothe the sloping shoulder,
deer overrun – oh aching lovely animal! –
while other forms, recognisable
or monstrous, move among close groves
of old oaks, tangled undergrowth.

Orderly my capital
is a neat small town
with an adequate high street:
butcher, post office, fishmonger
('they say fish be good for the brain'),
baker, fruit and vegetable stall.
This place is self-possessed, not terrible,
placid, domestic, quiet,
sensible shoes, but ah my dear,
what prophet ever came from here?

Periodically a crack appears
in the bland surface,
disturbing the reasonable peace.
The smiling face creases, breaks
in critical upheaval.
('Really, it's most uncomfortable.'
'It's treason, that's what!')
There's a radical flaw somewhere.

Berserk rage sparked by irritation
at a small rejection shocks all –
me too among the women shopping
appalled as this disowned wild bull
bolts down our street.

Blizzard, snow, no road, no goods:
damp miasma of loneliness,
lacking the faculty of connection,
wallows inert in squalor,
cannot even dress.

And the reverse, supply loads:
gladness when the dancing fit comes on –
what social joys are there,
what delicious lust! –
and the party goes.

Outburst, withdrawal, bounty:
anarchy, strike, carnival,
are the importunate intrusion
of that unacknowledged country
or insistent summons to it,
where every poet must journey,
alone in littleness get lost,
discover, return to tell.

1983

153

DOORMAT UNDERDOG

Humble hairy
nutbrown cheery
day in day out
patiently mute
I lie by the door
waiting for you to come.
> Trample on me;
> wipe your feet.
> Give me more, more
> of your adorable dirt.
> I am your doormat:
> home sweet home.

Till one day
when Super Heavy
stamped on it
it got some bottle
rocked intoxicated
hiccupped and slipped.
> Mr Big staggered
> and slumped flat.

Triumphantly
plumping to a hump
in the middle
the lumpen doormat
reared up enormous
into a shaggy dog
> poked its nose out
> sniffed sunshine, smiled.

Then woof!
down the road
galloped ecstatically
barking for joy
off to the park
to join the world:
      'I'll never be a hearthrug
      till I die!'
There was
a great dictator
till the saving grace
of good riddance
stirred the flutter:
Up to us!
      Among trouble and stress
      we have our moments.

THE GATECRASHER

Suddenly at the party
bison is there.
I am threatened
by his heavy leather body
sprouting matted wool.
He flanks me,
he corners me,
he interrupts.
Slit in his ample furry brow
stern steady eyes
hypnotise me with terror.

From his hieratic horns
descends condemnation,
tense black snakes
quill-barbed by porcupine
pricking bone to the quick,
head to tail ring-a-roses
enclose me in a monstrous encampment.
I am fenced in.
I become nuclear.

Beyond the coils recede
The party's other people.
They are noise far away.
They are top of the pops on telly.
I call for help, I shout.
No one can hear me
bullishly overlorded.
I am muffled.
I smell of him.

I try to outreach his shadow.
No one touches me
through the prickly seething
poisonous serpentines,
which they feel I am.
Isolated,
savagely wounded,
split,
I lethally explode.

Uninvited bison,
you arrive so quietly
on your dainty cloven hooves.
A party's not the time
to come to terms.
Yes, we will
but must defer it.
Wait till I summon you
in your infernal byre.

If you loom again
as importunate catastrophe,
before you get on top,
I'll bolt to the sweet heather cliffs
by that lit silvery sea,
sit there and breathe deep.
Then by the sun and moon
and all the earth's goodness
and by human loving kindness,
when I go back in,
hellborn bison, be gone.

AN EXORCISM

After the death, transplanting
and in that bitter soil
of love's utter denial –
it would be better
if you never were –
the young sapling
sipped at its taproot venom.

But something still insists:
I will exist;
neither father nor his new wife
shall take my life.
She kept it to herself
in secret furious grief
and became a socialist.

Stood with the oppressed
in poetry, translation,
what adult skill she had,
gave another tongue
to spread the word.
But lost her simplicity
of original identification.

Tainted sap stunted her knowing,
from dank unlove leafmould
drank diurnal self-loathing:
I am all wrong, wrong
also by class, by nation.
Thus father and wicked queen
maintained their stronghold.

'Free us from the yoke
and give us liberty'
was her English
for that cry from a far country
rid of a dictator.
Heard their singing
and howled.

The long-term prisoner
tortured in her rebelled
in surprise riot
raged at all – singers too –
an indiscriminate tantrum,
herself appalled,
bewildering them.

But they'd hit the high tower:
hot sweet music melted its shutters,
let her see,
purely topnotes lasered its locks,
set her free,
brought all that back to life,
wildchild to self,
outcast to company.

ANARCHANGELS

Swiftly they came
the anarchangels,
honey and lime
voices releasing
in naked duende
earthly heaven's desire,
swooning the senses,
prickling the nipples,
pressing lips, luring wombs
to wildness and folly,
but with power of the spirit
much more disturbing
than bodies attracted
and sonorous magic
transforming the planet
by reaching the core.

Yet they were human.
One was a chieftain
with massive charisma:
El Toro Corazón Arriba,
towed a beautiful girl,
publicly his
to mark his position.

One had an excellent mind
for discerning and teaching,
quick-witted, funny
and gifted at conversation,
with women was
mariposa de ñeques:
the mighty butterfly.

160

One a giant panda yearner
for his lost soporific sun
lay for hours on his back
singing along to his walkman
(Brandenburgs, opera),
barked when bitten and sulked,
magnetically drew through simplicity.

Wine made one declamatory
till his voice croaked –
uncelestial – but his face
might have been sculpted
serenely in stone
by peasants – he was one –
of his own country.

And their pure strong singing
was transcendental, inspiring a passion
of faith in the rightness
of what they were saying,
such attachment to their cause
that sometimes it sharply
angered and frightened
for what it demanded,
shaking foundations,
disrupting set patterns,
probing weakness and conflict,
unleashing repressions, self-questionings,
testing souls, to final exhaustion.
Swiftly they went
the anarchangels
and we were all changed.

THE DANCE

On grassy velvet
two gazelles
liquid eyes ecstatic
to the quick pulse
of thumping music
and their hearts uppity
whirl and stamp
fling out limbs
clasp each other
interweave
laugh in exultation
jubilantly whoop.

Tender girls
just fifteen and graceful
in this allegro outbreak
with all the original
power of maidens
long hair flying
slender windswept
frizzy silver birch
by a brown sunlit pool
in antiphonal rejoicing
reflections responding
each confirming both.

'Come on mum!'
Dance of three
in an intricate plait
(years of: do my hair,
no, that's not tight enough,
oh, you're hopeless at it;
tonight: we are women,
we are strong).
Can together
then the mother
prefers to sit a bit
revelling in them.

LIKENESS

Mother makes a demand,
the daughter flares,
sparks off the mother,
both rage: two fires
match each other,
blazing eyes engage
in fierce heat, in hate.
Yet these are loved faces
and their equal anger
flashes awareness
forcing each to admit
how alike, how close
they are, so many ways.
Feeling foolish as mere mirror
fury falters and fades out.

He's coming round
in half an hour,
announces the daughter
and gets in a flap
in the kitchen.
The mother lends a hand.
Of course we'd never
tidy our lives up
for a man! How low!
They grin.
He arrives with flowers
and urgent political action.
She is fifteen and beautiful.
The mother prays: enjoy
and treat each other well.

164

The daughter becomes kinder
to her not quite decrepit
old lady, tries to converse
with the shy man whom later
her mum in turn introduces.
No need to spell out
how they feel women
hold the world in common.

LUNAR

Cat-tangled hank of wool,
tensed to a nest of adders,
red seething coils.
Just one that slithered from bracken
across a sunny childhood path
stiffened the little intelligent pony
horrifically still, girl nearly unseated.
Her entrails today are a pile of vipers
in a deep hissing pit,
whose demon voice nags on and on.

Not that her interminably
drizzling complaint,
her slow massive anger
are at all unreal.
She does feel like that,
pain and all the poisonous unlove
of a thousand and one months
back to the original ten dark moons.
She does not feel the good;
it shuddered to a halt and bolted.

The destroying voice won't stop
accusing one who is there
till she is certain
he will bolt too,
almost wishes he would.
Bitten, envenomed,
some died of wounds.
Would hobnailed booted Hercules
wrestle the uncountable serpents,
stamp on their heads, hold on?

They dissolved next day
to blood and fell away.
Alone in the peaceful afternoon
she rests, washed out,
taking her time to recover,
soon one soft luxurious way
to be together darkly; sunrise,
daystar visiting, hero shining,
being the annunciatory
beyond saying, other.

NEW SONG

The woman was competent,
she was coping.
She did not know it
but she was starving
empty till you nourished me
with your hot broth
of delicious loving,
with which she slept
and awoke from deep
to far off forgotten
euphoric wellbeing.

She was earth mother
to son and daughter.
She did not crack
but she was parched
till I drank from you
first water and wine later,
white kisses and red
and the rosebud burst.
She slept and awoke fresh –
having been scorched, dust-laden –
sprouting vigorous May green.

She got up early
called to alarm
but shivered inside
shrivelled and cold
till you held me warm
in enormous arms
and your love amazed me;
don't foxes scavenge and flit afraid?
He stayed, and when he came
she could not have told
herself from him.

She was efficient
but taut and shrill,
vibrated off key
a lonely smell.
For a barely tolerable while
she lost her song,
made lists, took notes
but could not write.
Nothing recharged her energy
to abundance beyond survival
and she lacked the will.

Blunt-featured,
blond-furred,
low-throated animal,
large shambling ruminant,
surely present,
heard her poems
and understood;
what she hoped to give
generously did receive.

She listened too
and they both enjoyed,
met in a stream of language
babbling through dapple-dark wood,
partly unstrange as dreamt,
though all matchlessly new
and actual not make-believe.
But I never imagined it led
to open ocean of love.

OLD STORY

OVER

Love and trust
were limpid heather honey,
buttercups and daisies
open to the sun.

When it fell
to treachery
there lay a pool of butter
slippery on the floor,

who having lost
his shaping soul
was unkind
monstrously.

Blond bullock bounce
gallop and frolic dance
all joy and innocence
turned just like that

to savage damager
crashing about the republic,
whose cruel butts and kicks
kept upping the torture

till demented
she taunted
ranted
and he charged straight at her.

What had been love
in both became fury.
it was the darkness
of the same energy.

Now it is all over,
all poured out.
My cup is empty and dry.
I am my own.

It is bone china,
translucent, strong and delicate,
teatime familiar,
sound as a bell

drifting
spirit-stripwash blue
through childhood woods
in April,

tolling relief
for the passing,
recalling to life
goodwill.

OUT

At worst drop dead,
though we seek oblivion
for pleasure every night
in sleep like dying,
sometimes in drinking wine.
Warmth's abrupt withdrawal
calling up enormous
inky dogs of fear
stopped well short of killing,
just heralded a bad winter
of blood on snow, recessional
season of mauling.

She had accorded him power
and licence to lessen her.
Now to reclaim her own,
refuse to play the game
of who loves less
keeps more, is tactical
superior, yes! the winner.
Sudden denials dwindle him
to littleness, his loss.
Let him shrink, run pale,
send him to the jumble sale.
Think about a new spring dress.

MIDDLEMOST

Within the outer circle
the inner
and there
what had been
the learning haven
became the unspeakable
sleek black nightmare
the appalling pounding
sudden squad car
uniformed men
having huge power
hustling one off alone
to abomination of desolation.

The outer circle
has a long lake with ducks on
parkland grass and trees
bandstand wafting tunes
then you cross to the inner.

The inner circle
flaunts the brilliant garden
crimson roses creamy
some memory-scented
stripy lawn with daisies
ornamental water
where willows dip
to kingcups and lilies
and a shallow curve of poplars
at whose feet fuchsias bow
shelters the central fountain
piled with mer people.

Mirror of the soul
where an opulent grim hall
with howling chandeliers
houses the horror
heart of darkness
on the inner circle's rim

but within that
the garden glories
flagrant with red-hot pokers
subtle with mallow and cranesbill
tame squirrels to talk to
and oh the oceans of roses
peace and grace abounding.
Quick in the middle
leaps the fountain
to sit still by
and feel love well.

THE CHANGE

Inside that tight brown bud
what gummily goes on?
It is the chrysalis
where soft-ridged grass-green worm
curls to a small spiral,
ultimate masochist, foetal caracol
and in an enchanted coma
is reduced to dust.

Such perilous last analysis
conjures a transformed creature,
who will have her bliss
in time struggle free,
dry, flutter, fly up –
O colour! O my desire! –
lay her eggs in fullness,
briefly be it, utterly.

HEART IN PILGRIMAGE
1967-89

BEGINNING

SOPHIE MUTTERS AT THE DUSTBIN

'In the beginning was the word.'

JOHN 1:1

Yes worship the word,
always worship the word.

Once I almost went to bed
with a man who told me
about Arabic gutturals.
And in Berlin I nearly died
when this voice of iron and purest vowels
pronounced *die Schlüterstrasse*.

But the word to want
is the precison of a new thought,
intellectual and delicate
as cuckoo pint,
consoling and fragrant as resin,
press of the orange just at the point
where your prince of poppy is cool as logician.

It's a drag and a bad business
to make love when it's not a language.
Civilised idol of silver or gold
never heard with its ears
or cried in its throat.

Better scrap the sapless image
and worship the word.

179

THE PRACTICAL HOUSEHOLDER

'Without it nothing was made.'

JOHN 1:3

He converts his house
into a paradise
with tips from the *Observer*.

'Why are you always moaning
woman?
Can't you see
I am knocking this wall in
for open plan fucking
with colour tv?'

'Let me live
in a cave
with the prophet Elijah.'

Well, Elijah spoke his soul
by killing the prophets of Baal,
which was a touch wasteful.

The practical householder
converts his orange box
into a set of clocks.
Tick tock. What better way
to fritter the day
than the thrifty
hammer?

'But darling
look at the work
I am doing.
I am no longer young.
Was I ever clever?
I am a clerk.
How can I talk?
Don't you see
the house is me?'

'Yes.
God what a mess.
I loved your face.'

ELIJAH THE PROPHET

'There was a man sent.'
JOHN 1:6

1

Elijah said, 'I alone
am left a true prophet
and the prophets of money
four hundred and fifty men.
Let us see which party
can call down fire
upon the altar.'

The many money prophets shrieked and capered
and cut themselves with knives as is their custom.
At noon Elijah mocked them,
'Cry louder. Is he not a god?
ki elohim hu
Perhaps he is having a catnap
or has turned aside to pee.'
So they louder cried
but no one replied, no one answered,
no one heard.

At the time of the oblation
Elijah the prophet took twelve stones,
repaired the altar Jezebel
had broken down.
And when he prayed
the fire fell
and all the people were afraid
of their desire.

182

2

Elijah the prophet
sat down in the desert
and prayed that his spirit
might die.

He was sad,
sated with troubles
and slated the Lord
with many gutturals:
rabh 'attah jahveh

He slept
but the angel
made him wake,
gave him water and cake.

He was able to walk
in the strength of that food,
forty days, forty nights,
till he came to the mountain of God.

TAT'S SET UP

'The word was embodied and set up among us.'
                                    JOHN 1:14

In the red mud country
which he loved
he wrote stories
for company
in the loneliness,
not this stream of consciousness
but stuff for a good read.
With the blessed memory
of Emily, Charlotte, Jane,
he weighed his merits,
pardoned his offences,
kept pigs and lived
like a gentleman.

In Bristol
portly and provincial
reflected constantly
on his positiol,
this judicious choice
eschewing each excess.
His solid product was philosophy,
he had a system to defend,
a way of life to recommend.
He was a citizen
of no mean city.

184

London crammed him
and upset his stomach.
Aching on tarmac,
solo and claustrophobic,
he confessed the poem,
blew the bamboo flute.
Rootless, footloose,
an exact aesthetic
in his pocket,
this thin gipsy then
unsettled men and many
women with the sound
of his mind.

1967

WASP

It makes you sad
that death won't wait
till it is wanted
or appropriate
and that every private progress
suffers the irreparable loss.

This loss
you said
has been restored
by the risen Lord,
risen indeed.

Yes ah yes,
but did he do it?
Seeing the need of it
let us delight
in the thought of it.

But that gives us
no right
to construct
a structure like this
or to expect
the resurrection of the dead.

1967

MARTHA'S MARANATHA

Father, I was on my knees
polishing. Turning
to the telly
I found I had bowed down
to worship it.
Father, bless me.
Yes, smashing it
was fun
but life without it
needed resignation.

Wisdom in megalopolis
is to have broken all idols,
settling consciously
for a qualified unhappiness.

It is absurd
to rely
on a comic
spit in the eye
for the guard
and a promise
sounding meaningless.
We hope the joke
won't be sick.
Come Lord.

1969

DECEMBER

December ebb
the babe
turns the sun
back here.
From nadir
flows the new one
against fear
to grab
a new occasion.

To us the child is born,
winter gift
springs on us
a future season.
In return
the polar oldster scarlet
with white phylacteries
and parents daft
with pleasure press

the crude, the deft,
their earnings and their services
on the small champion,
and with enormous
lack of thrift
one day, last gift,
they die and pass
the parcel on –
adult dominion.

They disappear,
hand over earth and space
and whether
the darkness
is nothingness,
a waiting
or other living,
leave here
not knowing.

1974

MARCH

In the pressure
of that moment
of half light stillness,
O earth acceptable
I love you

and fellow creature,
natural here
though vulnerable
in all your opportunities
for sweet content,
I admire you.

I half suffer,
sorely want
the intellectual order
of such fine energy,
that beauty's shapeliness
strictly true.

Glimpse of the glory
when the species
finds fulfilment,
because humanity,
your known predicament
enables you.

For every god
your word has made
is only an interim
programme
and the scope to this
awareness
green friendship

between human beings
in grown intent
to dispossess our father
pain of his throne
Jack, and let joy take over,
help and hope.

1974

SPANISH SUMMER

She kneels curled,
like the unborn,
the young broad bean.
He will be revealed
from the tabernacle.
Coloured window
behind the altar,
crude figure,
still protest. Now
the improved idol
will be manifest,
sunlit dustily
embracing her,
prey her growling belly
crouches over.

Brass disturbance
thunders to assure
the populace.
Through the square
the villagers, after
their priest, monstrance
held high, approach
the church. The march
is a martial anthem,
trumpet and drum
serving to diffuse,
confuse *fiducia*
in the bread of their mass
with the dictator
of more questionable grace.

Stiffly Elizabeth
left her devotion,
went out in the sun
to see the band.
Spare thy people Lord,
who have been betrayed
often. Certainly she cared.
Deprivation and pain
all so untidy.
Surely some simplicity
waiting to be found
could stop it. Oh understand
with her own rainbow insight,
straightway (She is She) set right –
no longer be dismayed.

    Squat village inn with verandah,
    meandering foreign stream
    in a corner of Spain warmer,
    though rather like Devon,
    her damp now dream-crammed home.
    Not what she would expect.
    Bullrushes a frog Eden,
    ashbud sooty, erect
    from their biscuity flattened
    matted leaves overborne.
    Cloven hoofprints baked in mud
    hard to walk on in thin soles
    at the gaps in the bank
    where cattle go down to drink.
    Lanes overhung not all
    with flowers unknown,
    dog rose and honeysuckle

between fields of barley,
ripening earlier but still,
as she made Maria repeat:
Barley is bearded,
that's how you tell it from wheat.

Maria her pupil, aged twenty
and two years older than her,
accepted with meek adulation
(though beard was weird) this bullying.
She adored this saint who frowned
so much in church and knowing
such wisdom taught so patiently.
Timidly at night she would whisper
in her new plain English:
Do you want to be a nun?
Elizabeth unclear whether God
was herself, her dead mother,
swoony lover to be, popish plot
or what, kept quiet.
Maria rebuffed wept.

'All wired up here – pity,'
she said on their next walk. Startled
by this new titbit from on high
Maria looked softly receptive. Push.
'Obvious you can't ride across it fast.'
Snubbed again. Oh dear, why can't
she answer back? Slide past.
In memory she was a small girl
led by her father on Gold Rush,
galloping a tiny pony,
climbing huge Devon banks like an ant,

flying ditches, clinging on,
because to him she daren't
show fear at any obstacle.

They lay by the stream in clover.
Taste it. For the pupil initiation
for once comprehensible, though still
an odd English lesson,
the honey real to her. Smile.
Elizabeth rambled on to the Trinity,
how there are three persons in one nature,
each distinct but fully possessing it,
how through centuries intractable
muddle was wrought towards clarity
by heroic thought, how great Athanasius
escaped at night by boat,
how the divine word was humanity.

The turmoil seemed her own, the clanging bells –
confounded with all the church bells
she felt she had heard
as a small child at the end of war,
perhaps she had just been told –
street fighting at Ephesus,
seemed the excitement of her brain
pressing for her release.
She had read that contemplation
plumbs nothingness. She stripped
(it was hot) with diligent idleness,
the world slipped, she slept.
Let her rest: should we detest
those seeking purity and truth
however horrid and uncouth?

1974

195

FLAT

I was lack lustre,
tight as an oyster
locked on no pearl,
a soulless shellfish –
no self so a selfish consumer.
In my lust after knick knacks,
wherever I went
parcels would cluster.

My tense discontent
and patacake chatter
shattered the peace
and sucked up the silence
like a Black Hole
(trade mark of the new model
Superstar Vacuum Cleaner –
see recent *Which* supplement).

Venomous jelly,
frightful Medusa,
now I had become
the female extreme
form of unfreedom,
my quick snack persona
tasted unwholesome,
bitter and dull.

1983

SHINING

Double Helix

Sometimes comes stillness.
It is not ecstasy
now that her breath
breathes with the earth,
now that she grows in her
all living growth,
shape of that huge beech,
sunlit treescape wholly let be,
sweep of pure heaven;
redness of that late rose,
neither contralto crimson
nor a startling scarlet
but flush of its own luscious
reddy pinkish self between:
now that she's with each animal,
catness of that cat
blissful and fat in the sun;
and with people, human life
both smooth with delicious youth,
electric in mental strife,
and experienced, marked with memory,
scarred or well-worn, each line
of laughter, age or exhaustion,
the droop of bitterness,
glow of joy and continual
conflict between them:
'I know, I feel, I am.'

It is not ecstasy,
not outside but in with,
call it instatic, synstatic
(but that is jargon) I-you-we,
suspended conjugation,
momentary truce,
peace, an oddly matter of fact
self-evident tenderness.
It is a shining,
glory of being, worship,
in which she deeply rests
though she is not asleep.
Sometimes the shining speaks to her,
solicits, and since it is
what many have called God,
it seems it summons
to acknowledge him,
stroking her soul, cajoling:
Taste and see, I am good.
True, but God is not the name
of this epiphany.
She resists the labelling,
she will not bow down to him
who is not. Shamelessly she'll say,
blaspheme, as every human being
in this condition may
and must: 'I am who am.'

But not monist: we are many.
Although alike, unique,
individual in similitude,
each one of us separate
yet we are together here
by what we have in common,
what we share and share the more
by closeness, contact, word,
even in the writing of the dead.
Poetry is a word-shining,
consubstantial with that other
and worth striving for.
She was attracted to it
when the logic of theology
led through incarnate word
to godlessness and setting free.
Poetry is language memorable
through pleasure and shock of exact telling,
such a lot of living on this planet,
teeming too with other species,
so rich, so much, so beautiful,
place for the human race
to struggle for survival
and stroll its delightful garden.
The shining of it in stillness
and the power to make poetry
comes and goes like the English sun.

Words fail in emptiness,
the bravest quail
and poetry does not occur
with no receiving ear.
Fingertips press, words want to touch,
breathe, sigh, kiss, lips reach
and the spirit itself intercedes for us
with unutterable groans.
Thus the blessed trinity
is made in the image – swap –
of the human dynamic,
technically, circumincession:
I 'am' flows into 'speak' flows
into 'love' flows into being more
and so on round it goes.
Or call it the dialectic
between self and the utterly other.
Solitary becomes intolerable,
yet other spells danger, self loss,
anonymous threat.
The making of that other bodiless,
creating god by imagination
was a frantic swipe to snap
insufferable tension, stop
the restlessness we must endure
as the truth of our human state
and in illusion rest secure.

'My God, my God!' She battered at the door,
crying for him at night, sleeping on the floor.
Her parents threw her out for turning catholic.
No doubt she was also a pain in the neck.
Search, trial, pilgrimage.
In London dallied with smelly cabbage
(very holy that) in a shared bedsit
with a patient friend. As a nanny in Spain
read John of the Cross and Teresa,
mistress of contemplation.
Back again wanting to copy them.
Fragrance of apples and rain,
carmelite convent at home in autumn,
not very Spanish in fenland September.
Morning mass in the French church,
where the priests had liturgical hands,
Lauds in Leicester Square,
Vespers anywhere (phone boxes sometimes)
with a fellow enthusiast,
donkey work for a catholic publisher,
preaching lunchtimes at Charing Cross,
Sundays in Hyde Park,
celebrating the great *exultet* together,
the shining night of Christ our passover.
Then to study in Innsbruck
under renowned theologian.
God was not there.

There was another shining, ecstatic
exactly this time, that is another shone
as the living gold vermilion
deep fire at the core,
to which she now was drawn
out of herself, enraptured, unwilling,
to an alien centre,
heart given, pride gone, dependent,
spun round this fellow creature
as a feminine. absent-minded,
mild and obedient moon
locked on its course by passion.
Though bewildered, indeed astounded,
she was also relieved at the self-offloading.
That occasion was a melancholy youth
just down from Cambridge, ambitious,
brilliant, thrilling, a bit pompous
sometimes, to tell the truth,
bossy, with a glossy black forelock
he tossed and eyes dark liquid brown
that reminded her of her old pony.
The point is not to give an account
of that marriage to someone actually not her
(awkward and savage fact in disagreement),
merely to mention a day
dawned flat and grey when the glory
had long since faded away.

Shining came again, sun after rain,
either solitude resonant
or outward to haloed hero,
though not the same one: a succession.
Is this a trick of nature
giving a short spell
to establish breeding behaviour,
as at a quiet death they say
the earth shines too?
But when she leaps with the rainbow,
salutes the restored heavenly blue,
this is not cowlike declares her soul.
True, desire narrows attention,
ignores what it finds irrelevant,
but then love may follow
and with its tender clarity
discover, accept the whole.
A person may shine for us
but we do not choose who,
when or how long: it is a bonus,
just as we cannot order stillness.
Both gold glows come and go.
Meanwhile we can only continue
lives that thrive on affection,
work, speak, keep faith with humankind,
suffer, offer, maybe poetry
and endure all weather to the end.

Then again, without warning, vision:
'You, love, joy in your person.
Your body delights me utterly
and you fuck like an unfallen angel.
Your time is my time,
I kiss you with the mouth of my womb.'
And their continual conversation
was very pleasant to her.
He told her about molecules and algae
and diving expeditions he went on
off his Sicilian coast.
He read her Dante and cooked spaghetti
boasting disgracefully about the sauce.
His hands were animal competent
at handling wood and other material.
It was a bitter quarrel
when he wanted to live in Milan, she London.
At that doom, five of her teeth fell
like a nightmare of solid tears,
the first late at night in that hell hole
of looming fears, the bus stop at Archway.
He did not shine now,
he was a burning. She fell ill
having given herself away, become
unwelcome, lumpen, lost in such distress
that stillness found no place
to visit her and heal.

The machine did not break down.
She kept house, fed children daily,
taught a bit but could barely translate,
though it was their bread and butter,
and virtue of poetry almost gone.
At last she began to recover,
when she let go and stopped being angry,
was released when she released,
blessed and asked a blessing.
Now when the boon of stillness comes,
its embrace is wider
and the golden afternoon more generous.
The visitations form a spiral,
parallel and interwoven with that other,
the strike of erotic attraction.
Both are moments of brightness
in a winding cross-linked chain,
ground of being, not supernatural,
no, but structure of all the living,
DNA molecule, the double helix.
Complex? Well, in the science museum
look at the lovely coloured model.
In exasperation, the gipsy woman
stood up like a thing possessed,
drank without pause the fire-water brandy
and sang with duende. It could not last
but it *was* the marvellous rose.

1983

EASTER

The myth of the word,
incarnate in Jesus,
god in us,
how he sided with the poor
against the powerful,
bringing them his gospel,
making common cause.

The myth of god human in Jesus,
arrested, condemned,
how they tortured,
how they killed him,
church and state,
for preaching the gospel to the poor,
siding wholly with them.

The myth of his rising
on Easter day,
springing all glorious,
how he talked to his friends,
making his case
against the powers of darkness,
vindicating his gospel to the poor.

Though abused, exploited for death,
this is nevertheless a true myth
declaring the crucial truth:

The power of good in us
we abstracted, called it god,
an absolute on high upheld.
Then god came down to earth,
born of a woman.
Because his gospel was a scandal
the evil idols struck to kill.
He was crucified but life prevailed.

When he rose most beautiful,
god restored to a body fit,
his proper immanence and shape,
he showed the human form divine
and human good greater than evil.
But he did not hand over the kingdom
to the Father. He stood up
and god in heaven had to abdicate.

Utopian hope, imagined good
are wholly within the human scope.
Nowhere but in us is god,
as is the deepest pit of hell.
We choose which side to be on.
The gospel of the incarnate word
prefers the poor to the powerful.
The rising means the mighty are put down.

1983

207

AGAINST IDOLS

Love's denial is hate.
Hope lost is unbelief,
despair of all relief.
Faith's opposite: idolatry.

An idol is a false god
which demands and feeds on death.
It does not need to legitimate
itself: touch it you die.

Sin is what kills people,
with weapons wickedly quick
or slow dearth neglectful,
perhaps proud of maximum profit.

Sin is mortal not because
it kills the soul (though it does).
Sin follows foul idols,
physically kills many.

Don't look to god above
to break the dolorous lords.
Be your own iconoclast,
shake free at last.

Faith in human good,
worded how best we can conceive,
that is god in us incarnate.
The baffled devils retreat.

1983

CHALCEDON

Not the gnosis of an elect
self–selected elite
calling their slight trendy insights
an exclusive enlightenment.
The principal part of speech is verb
and the word saves in time, becomes flesh,
submits to passion, shines in resurrection.
It speaks to all, of all for all;
it connects, it expresses the people.
Great or small it says how things are,
tells the truth strongly and sweetly.
It names wrongs, rages, castigates,
soothsays, praises, prophesies,
propounds possible harmonies,
earthly heavens, happy days.

It must do it well,
expertly, be superb;
it is not fluid conversation.
It is conceived alone
and when it arrives to be enrolled,
may be unwelcome, no room for it.
Pains have to be suffered at its coming,
which is hard labour, uncomfortable.
It must cost, strive for perfection
and then stop at that.

And one and the same body of words,
piece of work, doing, poem,
one subsistence, one hypostasis,
one voice, one face,
whose effect, like its existence,
is not all in the clouds,
no mere object of contemplation,
but which speaks on a historical occasion
(then again) and when it works
the power of its sound burns:

has not a single nature, *physis*,
it has two;
and is apprehended in two ways.
When we are gathered together
and it is uttered we hear it
and when I want to be quiet I read.
The latter as print, text in view,
though it is notation
of the noise of the other,
is yet a distinct nature,
unconfused, and the difference
in no way diminished because of the union
of one and the same subsistence –
word incarnate –
in two natures distinct not separate.

So let us celebrate
not cool detachment of the business spirit,
not the enrichment of a clique,
not gnosis of fashionable hierarchies,
not initiation into dominations, thrones,
to kick competitors and scale to the top quick,
not pseudo-enlightenment of name-dropping and cheap puns,
not spite, logic-chopping, profiteering,
not the appropriation of the wordhoard,
or the privatisation of any public treasure.

But in two natures one poem,
redeeming word, wisdom,
pouring itself out,
coming down,
kenosis, *katabasis*, harrowing of hell,
taking it all on,
to embody, suffer, transform
the whole, for the life of it,
for the healing
of the whole people.

1985

The Council of Chalcedon in 451 defined the saving incarnate word as one subsistence in two natures. Greek terms in the poem are *physis*: nature; *kenosis*: emptying; *katabasis*: going down.

HEART IN PILGRIMAGE

The warm circle broke
when a draught put out the light,
half heard groans, mutterings.
It is not right
this house should ride on backs –
one uncosied member thought –
of excluded humans crawling.

Pilgrim started in the dark,
left walls and with stars occluded,
all systems down, mere ache
to see, to love – not god but what? –
trod making many mistakes
the road to that
which was not yet.

A knapsack full of idols, household gods,
keepsakes, spoke with authority
of sacred father, city, kingdom.
They broke or hollow ones exploded
when friends made on the journey
fed in red fermenting wisdom.
The crash was most enjoyable.

The smashed up idols helped to make the track,
sharp shards but many pilgrims
stamped them in, crushed well,
till they became fragments, part,
dust of the ground to travel,
the road to that
which was not yet.

Then there were false turnings
and lush patches of sweetness,
deceiving tones which insisted: Easy.
Don't go on. I'll be your wholeness.
Insidious self-questionings
as the journey distressed children
requiring an inheritance of tradition.

But we couldn't stop in that house
built not on rock or sand but pain.
Now we have no places set.
Just times of knowing, particles, poems,
movable feasts, rests, wine
prophetic of that remaking
and moments of it with those we meet.

1985

OFFICE

Not religion, discipline.
Watch and pray
that you don't fall.
Make the poem well,
rehearse the voice,
practise technique
not to inhibit but set free.
A slight narcissistic conceit
touting mere popularity
is utterly out of place.
No duende will attend you,
tonight you juggle
in vain, you are trivial.
The glory has departed.

Not religion, discipline.
Watch and pray
that you can tell.
Such ascesis, idleness,
is to put your mind
in the right frame –
notice, listen, see,
then get it accurate
so that words not only fit
but illumine truly.
Bloodbeat, rhythm, flame –
let beauty burn.
Were not our hearts burning
when we heard?

The deep heat is a belonging,
heartflung fellow feeling,
cries, yes – yes – yes –
till wordlessness.

1985

MAGNIFICAT

Keeping faith
abolished the lofty nobodaddy,
impostor butler to our shortcoming,
as well as idolatrous crown (prop)
to upper class
and hierarchy, being top.

Ascending to put down
this posed legitimator of all lords,
chief mighty from his seat,
the word incarnate (god with us
and nowhere else)
cried with a human voice:

This is a stick-up
by the Earth Liberation Front
power to the people rising
for this christian story's point:
god riddance and fair sharing!

And the stars in their courses
heavenly bodies and planetary sisters
sang and matter's emergent properties
yearned in harmonies ear never heard
before then for fulfilment:

Evolution's hope the human species
becoming the best it ever guessed
and more, possessing heaven
first in imagination then getting it
down to earth to make it happen.

A loving sphere whose energy
spins delight not blighted lives not
massive pain and even when
everything has to be done
again and again and again
keeping heart.

1989

BLACK AND RED
1989

SITTING IT OUT

On the day when to its shame
an England of haves and self-servers –
couldn't care less
about others –
returned that snatcher
to saturation blitz us
in a massively dangerous third term,
when Walthamstow, Battersea, Fulham
fell to yuppie smugs,

the pathetic so-called fallacy
had a field day –
not so dozy – over the whole
country, over Gospel Oak
the heavens wept buckets,
roared and thundered
warning upon warning
and lightning zigzagged
over Highgate Pond.

Having summoned
the free people
to picnic on Parliament Hill
John Rety sat alone,
patiently waiting,
faithful, indomitable
now rather grumpy gnome
under a large umbrella in the storm.
O comrades come rally.

June 11th 1987

HEDGEHOG IN BABYLON

'I will make her a possession of the
hedgehog and pools of water.'
ISAIAH, *Oracle against Babylon*

Twice you withdrew
to the wilderness,
shaking the dust of the city
off your feet, angry prophet,
cursing us, cursing me,
because I was unjust,
flippant and permitted it
and, cardinal sin
in a fellow poet,

I had not listened well
to your strong hard pain,
systematic ill treatment,
alienation, abuse,
your mental hospital poem.
You told me my sympathy
was ideological,
only for the wrongs of women.
I felt deep shame.

But at times your polemic
was clogged and prosaic,
while some poems weren't ship canal
at all, but mountain brook,
pure lyric,
thrushlike potent echoing
rush of your native lament
through a dry kindling wit.

I begged you to forgive
if a noisy deaf spirit
brashly had made you bristle.
When friendship snuffled you
back to the tribe,
I saw with delight you sip,
cautious at first, then absorb
spicy hot rum esteem,
transform the tough-quilled porcupine.

And now let wise owls
of outlying West London listen,
wolves withhold their ululations
and the violent shelve their long knives.
For dearest of all I hear
clear union of what was split
fearlessly flower in fresh poetry
of a whole human animal
self in possession, in power.

PERFORMING

Poetry the darling child of speech and lips . . .
till it is spoken it is not performed,
it does not perform, it is not itself.

HOPKINS

Rise like lions after slumber
in unvanquishable number.
Shake your chains to earth like dew
which in sleep had fallen on you.

SHELLEY

Damp heavy dough,
a sticky mess,
unpalatable,
cold although afraid
of that mysterious process
which first would warm
in the airing cupboard,
gently make me rise,
then bake fierce and slow,
transform me into bread,
new feast for the table.
I resist but yes,
this it is
I want to become.

WORKING

Its function is to enchant.
First construct and then
utter in every detail
words exactly right
to cast a spell.
You cannot translate it
into a prose discourse,
as stripping a person
of a chain of office
does not just remove a decoration
but is a withdrawal
of that role and power.
And as a little guerrilla unit
violent only for its purpose
must keep time, be economical
to take a national palace,
nothing is superfluous
in the poem; it is there
as precise magic to count
in the incantation.

SURVIVING

Trees never stop growing
all their lives, you said.
But now in late November
hurricane-bereaved
of several airy branches,
whose strength was my joyful
breath and balanced me,
as well as suffering
my seasonal stripping of leaves,
I am dead tired,
slow, timid, holding off
the cold assault
with a must be tough-rooted
skeleton belief.

WOMAN OF EL SALVADOR

My strong sons,
sweeter than star apples,
both murdered,
all gone.

My firstborn,
I was just a girl,
his father vigorous, *guapo*
(we heard humming birds
where we lay
and afterwards ate mango),
a proud man,
straight coco palm,
like our son Humberto
when they gunned him down.

My strong sons,
sweeter than *chiche coyol*,
both murdered,
all gone.

And my little one,
my Coquito,
my clever monkey.
I nursed him long,
my last time,
till he was bored and naughty,
tweaking and nipping
so I let him go.
He was always impatient
to be a man,
foolhardy, accident prone.
But he was just thirteen,
a boy still, wiry liana,
when they gunned him down.

My strong sons,
sweeter than wild bee honey,
both murdered,
all gone.

> Must everything we cherish,
> nurture and watch grow
> fall to the destroyer?
> Why does their heavy hand
> smash all we have done,
> kill and kill and kill?
> They are cruel past all reason.
> It is beyond understanding.

I was a ripe calabash.
I shrivel like last year's almond.
I am an empty gourd.
I am stripped maize
but my harvest is wasted.
My arms hang slack.

I have seen their wanton destruction
go on and on and on,
my people's pain my own,
many mothers weeping for their children,
dead bodies piled like rubbish,
many sons and daughters
mothers fathers friends
all murdered,
all gone.
Let it end.

Chiche coyol is a drink made of palm juice.

MILK AND HONEY

Her milk glutted hungry babies,
she provided honey for tea
and the backs of her knees
were sticky like theirs,
the floor and the cat's fur.
They stuck to each other in a fluff
of familiar rhymes, puzzles, scuffles,
trodden wax crayons, secret games.

Though emerging's cumbrous enough surely
just finding your own shoes,
never mind a bevy of little ones
and every road unsafe,
the being stuck and the sagging
were rewarded a hundredfold
by the staggering sweetness
of her lambs.

But she was not a mature sheep
and could not be. Not only that
the human clothing offered
did not fit and she was unwilling
to grow into it.
Motherhood, yes –
came naturally – but otherwise
no programme microchip.

Woolly however in naivety –
intuitive but facile telescopic
overlooking the gigantic cost –
she half believed that human poems,
having superceded godseedword,
could harrow every devil out of hell
and when that ecstatic fling met lamb love
even the blue meanies join the dance.

Visions of innocence! Celebrations!
But mornings after were a long haul.
From busy viscous sloth
new poems peeped, took shape,
reappearing soul and prophecy
and words sometimes burst into action.
When visible results were few
hope disappointed and stubborn
staggered on because it had to,
that was all.

The marriage software package
crashed and love of men so mined
with tripwires everywhere
that women often did not bother
anymore, while for others
an occasional armistice
with wild beauty and bonfire
came and went, came and went.

Meanwhile her growing lambs
grazed these nomadic pastures
(though they stuck to the one house)
over mountains with sheer rock patches,
vertiginous crevices, till she awoke
one morning shocked to find them
reaching the age she had been
when her first was winterborn.

She salutes fellow adults
facing a far bleaker world
for all we failed, but at least we tried
and struggle on believing even stronger,
older, fiercer, now that evil openly
flaunts its gains, congratulates
itself this country is all wrong.
For the young who are not sold
it's doubly difficult.
Now this is staggering generosity.

They suffered our mistakes
and offer forgiveness.
They are commanded
to become decadent money machines
(many of their contemporaries succumb).
What deep relief and salve
to find they share the vision,
have loving souls, hope
and want to help
revolve a loving globe.

Simple perhaps, but otherwise this is hell
with no way out of it.
There is no other doorknob
to fit and turn the spindle
which can't open on its own
to that huge change
for which the world still groans.
Already in some modest threatened places
these groans have proved
that they were labour pains.

BALLAD OF NICARAGUITA

Yes, you are massively poor,
racing redblack for survival
and by that colossal ill will
crippled and mangled in war.

Of course we'll try to raise money,
resources you urgently need,
ashamed, not quite impotent, glad.
But we need your charity.

Our country runs sluggish and cold,
clogged with unlife called Profit,
drugged with unlove called Private.
You are heart of the heartless world.

Nicaragua you must survive
for your own sake and all the rest of us,
the comfortless unconfessed of us,
your rhythm keeps us alive.

The style of your revolution
has got it, the alchemical brew
mixing spice of life, sweetness too,
with militancy and passion.

Like a little pigeon, like a chinese lantern,
Nicaragua carries the guerrilla
and the military pilot pores over
his map with a girl of nine.

When you see those mountains' green green
you wish you could be a horse
and Carlos Fonseca's blue eyes
are short-sighted but have true vision.

Aware yet still ready to bless,
Tomas comes out of gaol
and his tortured hands are able
to keep all their tenderness.

Acknowledged, elected duly,
your legislator poets determine
the triumph of your revolution
is the triumph of poetry.

This Christmas London is cold,
conservatives wreck and rave.
Nicaragua you must survive,
hope of the hopeless world.

REVOLUTIONARY SINGER

Your singing is an urgency
of harsh unpent dark water
crashing on me, drenching,
strong-arm undertow making me go
along with its will.

Such a big voice
for that small body
nakedly astonishes.

It is an innocence
both primal and conscious
of evil but choosing
one great good with all
that has and will cost.

Its peculiar raucous animality
presses my heart so tight
I burst with tenderness.

RED

This red rag
is the rage of being
wind-tattered
fluttering triumphantly,

this same heart
is a strong pump
for the blood
rhythm,

energy beat,
sweet delight,
wine of living,
rose of passion.

But disappointed
womb stained
the rag red
lost child

and this young woman
was put behind glass
where not even her mother
could fold her

in strong arms
or kiss
and she receded,
lost voice.

Injustices need
shattering; noise
and sometimes bloodshed
cannot be avoided

to break out in song,
make chaos and undoing
breed and form
a glad new poem,

scarlet banners
of love risen,
rose of passion,
wine of living

circulating red.

EPILOGUE

REVENGE

My personal revenge will be your children's
right to schooling and to flowers.
My personal revenge will be this song
bursting for you with no more fears.
My personal revenge will be to make you see
the goodness in my people's eyes,
implacable in combat always
generous and firm in victory.

My personal revenge will be to say:
'Good morning!' in streets with no beggars,
when instead of locking you inside
they say: 'Don't look so sad!'
when you the torturer daren't lift your head.
My personal revenge will be to offer
these hands you once ill-treated
with all their tenderness intact.

And it was the people that hated you most
when song was of violent deeds
but the people under their skin
have hearts beating black and red!

Song by Luis Enrique Mejía Godoy
based on words by Tomas Borge, Home Secretary, Nicaragua
Translated by D. L.

SONG

Mistakes heartache
  unexpected defeat
burnt all black
  dead beat.
Fire charred the heath
  death dried the heart.
They who hated this earth
  have deeply scarred.

Yet deeper the seed
  love sheds its life -
Blood stopped stone dead.
  Moist warmth unfurls leaf.

  My hope is red petal
    heart beat.